SEW U
HOME STRETCH

ALSO BY WENDY MULLIN WITH EVIANA HARTMAN

SEW U

The *Built by Wendy* Guide to Sewing Knit Fabrics

SEW U
HOME STRETCH

The *Built by Wendy* Guide to Sewing Knit Fabrics

Wendy Mullin with Eviana Hartman

ILLUSTRATIONS BY BECI ORPIN

ADDITIONAL ILLUSTRATIONS BY KISS ME I'M POLISH: AGNIESZKA GASPARSKA, HOLLYE CHAPMAN

LITTLE, BROWN AND COMPANY | NEW YORK • BOSTON • LONDON

Copyright © 2008 by Wendy Mullin

Little, Brown and Company
Hachette Book Group USA
237 Park Avenue, New York, NY 10017
Visit our Web site at www.HachetteBookGroupUSA.com

First Edition: May 2008

Library of Congress Cataloging-in-Publication Data
Mullin, Wendy.
    Sew U home stretch : the Built By Wendy guide to sewing knit fabrics /
Wendy Mullin with Eviana Hartman ; illustrations by Beci Orpin ;
additional illustrations by Agnieszka Gasparska. — 1st ed.
            p. cm.
    Includes bibliographical references and index.
    ISBN 978-0-316-11837-8
1. Machine sewing. 2. Knit goods. I. Hartman, Eviana. II. Title.
    TT713.M847 2008
    646.2'044 — dc22   2007031531

10 9 8 7 6 5 4 3 2 1

IMAGO
Designed by Goodesign

PRINTED IN CHINA

DEDICATED

To Erin and Jason

CONTENTS

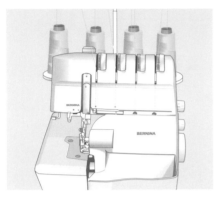

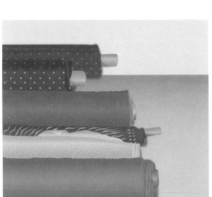

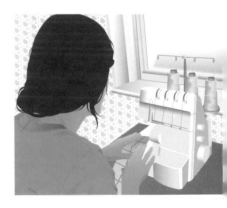

INTRODUCTION
STRETCHING THE TRUTH

Why Knits Are Easy and Fun

REMEMBER WHEN A T-SHIRT WAS JUST A HUMBLE T-SHIRT? TIMES HAVE CHANGED, AND IT'S TIME STRETCH FABRICS GOT THE ATTENTION THEY DESERVE.

Thanks to the general trend toward casual, easy day-to-night dressing, T-shirts and sweats are no longer just for lounging around the house. More and more of us are dressing head to toe in layers of knits. All of which means that designing and sewing with stretch fabrics can be every bit as creatively satisfying as working with wovens. Knits are an important part of my Built by Wendy collections—not just printed T-shirts and leggings, but also interesting silhouettes like draped tops, Empire-waist dresses, and more. Even ultra-high-end designers are treating stretch fabrics like wovens, creating clothes that utilize such elaborate gathering and layering that you almost can't believe they're made of T-shirt fabric.

Still, when most people think of sewing, they probably imagine an elderly tailor hunched over with a tape measure around his neck, pinning together a crisp wool suit or couture dress. They probably don't envision an ordinary person whipping up a bathing suit, a T-shirt, or a pair of panties. When I first started sewing, I gravitated toward rigid woven fabrics like cotton shirting and denim, because knits seemed so mysterious. I remember dissecting my T-shirts as a teenager, trying to understand how they had been stitched together. I'd go to the fabric store and wander around in bewilderment, unsure of where to find fabric to make that distinctive stretchy rib collar.

My first experience working with knits was altering my favorite rock T-shirts (this was in the 1980s, before every band was producing cute girl-friendly fitted tees). I would shorten them, cut off the necklines, and slim down the side seams. When I managed to make my beloved Smiths shirt fit perfectly, I knew I was on to something. I started playing around with knits and realized that they were actually *easier* to sew than wovens. Instantly, I got hooked on making jersey tank tops and baby-doll T-shirt minidresses. I couldn't believe I could crank out a T-shirt in only an hour! Still, I was a bit ahead of my time. A couple of years ago, a friend complimented my T-shirt, and I excitedly responded, "I made it!" She looked dumbfounded and said, "What? How do you *make* a T-shirt? That is so strange." In fact, when I told friends that my second book would be about knits, most of them immediately responded, "Oh, those are really hard to sew, right?"

It was then that I remembered how I felt when I was a novice sewer. For some reason, stretch fabrics still have the stigma of being scary. I had to explain to my friends that in fact working with stretch fabrics is a natural progression for the beginning sewer. Besides, knits are snuggly, soft, and a lot of fun to experiment with. You get to use a different machine—a serger—which trims, sews, and finishes your seams in one quick motion (you can also use your regular sewing machine; more about that later). Plus, with knits, the patterns and sewing are simple: no difficult buttons, zippers, or darts; very little use of complicated facings and interfacings. Once you're armed with a combination of basic pattern-making skills and useful fabric, trim, and stitching techniques, you'll have the freedom to get really inventive. And best of all, because they're knits, the pieces you'll make will be so comfortable that you'll wear them forever.

BOOK SMART
WHAT TO EXPECT

In this book, I'll teach you the basics of sewing stretch fabrics—skills that are rooted in the general sewing techniques of my first book, *Sew U*, but that are also knit-specific. I don't want to overwhelm you, so I've kept things at the beginner level, offering the tips and techniques that I feel, based on my two decades' exper ience, will give you the confidence to invent your own de-signs, and nothing more. (When I first got my serger, I was completely intimi-dated by all the stitches and thread variations that were covered in its manual. But over time I realized that there are just a few basic stitches I use constantly; most of those crazy advanced techniques are a waste of time and energy.)

As I did in *Sew U*, I will teach you about fabrics, cutting, and sewing. However, *Sew U* is a more comprehensive guide to the nuts and bolts of sewing and the process of getting set up, so I think it's a good idea for absolute beginners to read and use both books. Here I have included, again, some basic patterns and plenty of project ideas. You'll learn some easy pattern-making techniques to alter my pattern pieces into a variety of shapes, from basic tees to dresses, tanks to hoodies. You can follow my projects step-by-step or use them as a base for your own creative ideas. Through simple changes, such as altering a neckline or shortening sleeves, you can make dozens of different styles. And by customizing them even further with unique fabrics, trims, and stitching techniques—I suggest plenty of options for each, but you can do whatever you like—you'll have a whole new wardrobe. The possibilities are endless!

Of course, if you've read *Sew U* or seen my designs, you'll know I've never believed in playing totally by the rules. As part of my mission to demystify stretch fabrics, I will give you a few alternative techniques to make sure that no matter what materials you have to work with, you'll have a satisfying sewing experience. Ideally, I recommend that you use a serger for the projects in this book, but I give alternative instructions for those of you who use a conventional sewing machine. If you don't like or don't fit into the patterns provided, you can still apply my techniques to store-bought patterns of a similar nature—and I will show you how to make a simple T-shirt pattern based on your own favorite, perfect-fitting shirts. And in case you have trouble finding fabric or simply can't afford it, I will show you ways to recycle fabrics and combine elements from used or old clothing.

I hope you apply what you learn in this book not only toward making up your own designs but also toward altering patterns or clothing that you already have. I want you to take the pile of old T-shirts you were planning to send to Goodwill and think, "Wait—I can cut the neckline off this and sew it onto another shirt and make an entirely new shirt!" I want you to look at your brother's old gym-class hoodie and envision a cute, cozy winter dress. I want you to turn sweaters into scarves and leg warmers into sleeves. This book is more than an instruction manual—consider it a launching pad for your own creativity.

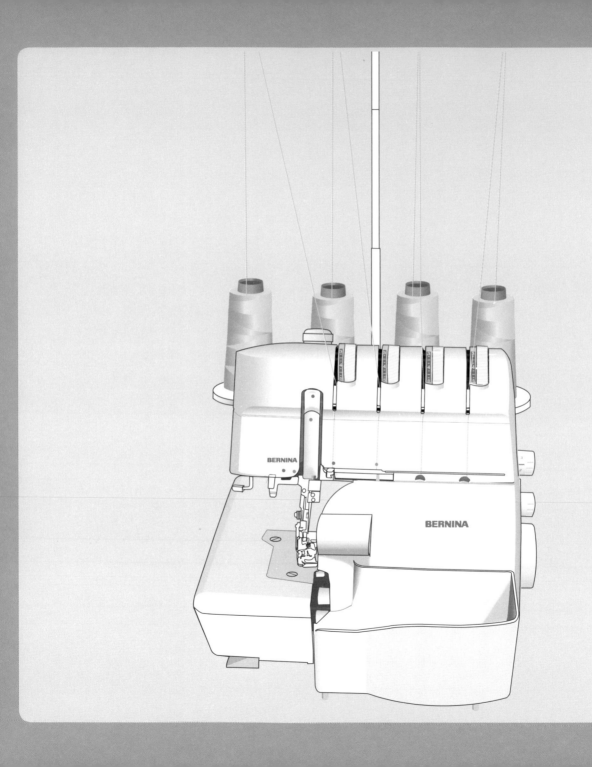

CHAPTER 1
SUPPLIES YOU'LL DEMAND

Getting Equipped to Sew Knits

JUST AS KNITS AND WOVENS ARE MADE DIFFERENTLY, SO ARE SOME OF THE TOOLS AND EQUIPMENT USED TO SEW THEM—LIKE A SCARY-LOOKING MACHINE CALLED A SERGER.

Of course, serger sewing *is* sewing, so many standard items you may have used for woven fabrics are also used for the projects in this book. Assuming you have already stocked our basic sewing kit (see my first book, *Sew U*, for a thorough guide), I've compiled in this chapter a list of everything knit-fabric-specific you'll need to get started. While I recommend a serger for these projects, I understand that not everyone can afford to splurge on one. (I sewed for twelve years until I ponied up for one myself.) With ingenuity, you can actually get by without all the knitcentric machinery and supplies, so it's up to you how pro you want to go. If you want to make a quick, cute top to wear out tonight that looks good on the outside but not so good on the inside (and you won't be devastated if a few stitches unravel on the dance floor), then follow the "Getting By" suggestions, culled from the tricks I learned as a struggling student sewer. If you are totally serious about sewing, follow the "Pro" suggestions. The more you sew knits, the more experience and confidence you'll have, which will help you figure out where you can fudge it and where you can't.

MACHINERY

Sewing stretch fabrics traditionally requires a machine known as a **serger** (also known as an **overlock machine**), which not only sews the seam but finishes and trims the edge in one motion. As the fabric is run through the machine, upper and lower knives trim the seam perfectly while the needles and loopers wrap threads around this trimmed seam. The finished seam actually stretches with the stretch fabric. (The serger, incidentally, can also be used for woven fabrics, either for sewing and finishing the seam or for just finishing the raw edge on a regular stitched seam.) On a **conventional sewing machine**, the equivalent of sewing a stretchy seam is using a zigzag stitch.

The serger can create a variety of overlock stitches for seam types such as overlock and flatlock using two, three, or four spools of thread. The appropriate stitch depends on the kind of fabric you're using and the purpose of the seam. Take a look inside one of your T-shirts and you'll see what an overlock stitch looks like. Compare this to a few stretch fabric items, such as a pair of underpants and a bathing suit. You will notice that each looks slightly different.

You can also use a serger to finish edges using special stitches, as opposed to turning back hems and topstitching them the way you would on your conventional machine. The serger can finish the raw edge of a seam with an overlock stitch, or it can finish the hem of your garment by covering the raw edge with a row of tightly looped threads, called a roll hem.

If you prefer the look of a proper hem that folds back and is topstitched, you will need a **cover-stitch** or **chain-stitch machine**. This machine creates a straight stitch on top and an overlock-looking stitch underneath in one motion. Take a look at the hem of your T-shirt: On the outside, you'll see two rows of straight stitching, and on the reverse side, you'll see an overlocked finished edge. The cover stitch stretches with your fabric, unlike a conventional machine topstitch: If you used the conventional topstitch for a stretch fabric hem and pulled on it, the entire hem would rip out! The cover stitch can also be used on wovens, but it is generally used for stretch fabrics.

Knit Picky: Which Machines Do I Really Need?

For the most professional-looking stretch fabric clothing, I recommend using a serger and a cover-stitch machine together. Of course, that is a lot of machinery and money—and there are ways to get by using just a serger, or just a conventional machine, or a combination of both. If you're a novice, I recommend starting out using your conventional machine for sewing knits. If you really get into sewing, then go ahead and invest in a serger. I think it's important for semiserious sewers to have both. Even when you're using your conventional machine for woven projects, you can use your serger to cover those raw frayed edges easily. Once you're sewing stretch fabrics regularly, then you'll probably want to invest in the cover-stitch machine. Some sergers can convert back and forth to the cover stitch, but I think they're sort of hard to deal with, especially when you constantly have to reconfigure your machine back and forth midproject.

The Serger

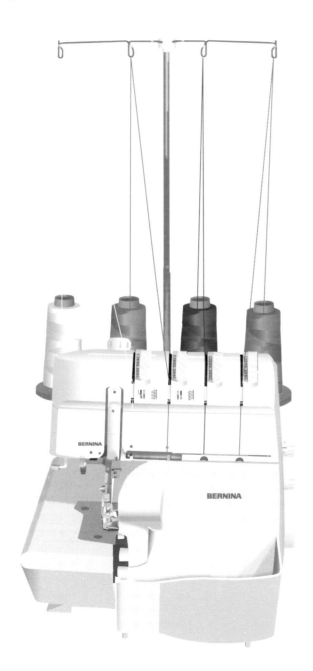

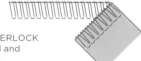

2-THREAD OVERLOCK
1 needle thread and
1 looper thread

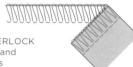

3-THREAD OVERLOCK
1 needle thread and
2 looper threads

4-THREAD OVERLOCK
2 needle threads and
2 looper threads

Getting By
Conventional machine set at zigzag

Recommended
3-thread overlock stitch using a basic serger for most of the projects in this book

Pro
Basic serger machine and cover-stitch/chain-stitch machine

The Conventional Machine

MOCK OVERLOCK

ZIGZAG

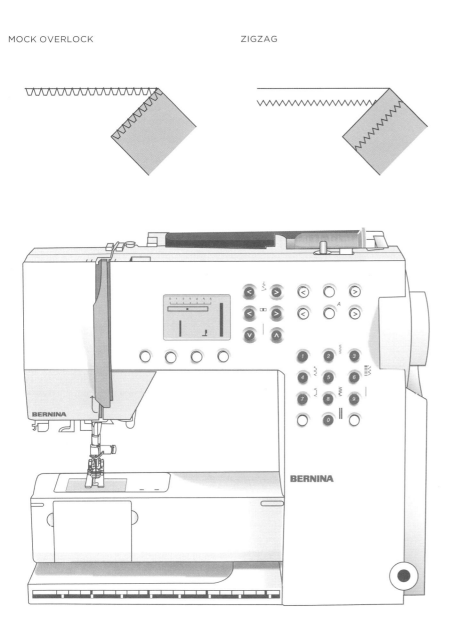

BERNINA

The Cover-stitch/ Chain-stitch Machine

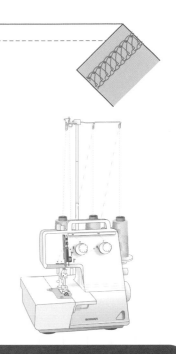

SIDE NOTE

The **chain stitch** is a straight stitch that is very durable and does not stretch very much. Therefore, to state the obvious, you won't really use it for the purposes of this book. Chain-stitching is used in areas such as the seams of your jeans: Look there, and you'll see a single line of thick stitching plus a serged seam that covers the raw edge of the fabric.

Shopping List

If you're sewing knits, you'll need a slightly different set of supplies than you will for sewing woven fabrics. The following knit-specific items are essential for the projects in this book, though it's also worth consulting *Sew U* for a thorough guide to stocking up.

Getting By
Universal size 12 needles (80 size)

Recommended
Ballpoint size 12 needles—great for sewing basic cotton T-shirt fabrics

Pro
Multipack of sizes 70–90 (aka sizes 10–14) ballpoint needles

STORAGE TIP

Label the wedges of your tomato pincushion by needle style and size. This will save you hassle when switching back and forth between projects.

NEEDLES

As with conventional sewing, with knits it's important to choose needles that are appropriate for the kind and weight of fabric and the type of thread you'll be using. Most sergers use one or two household-style needles, depending on whether you're using a 3-thread or 4-thread stitch, which are usually labeled under the 130/705H-S code system. Stretch fabrics, because of their nature, generally work best with a ballpoint-style needle (while wovens use a sharp needle), but a semi-ballpoint, universal-style needle is fine too. Most stretch fabric projects can use a size 70 (10), 80 (12), or 90 (14) needle. The lightest, 70, is good for delicate knits like silk jersey, while the heaviest, 90, is good for thick knits like polar fleece. If you're a regular sewer, you'll want to stock up on a range of options to avoid annoying last-minute runs to the fabric store.

When in doubt, try universal needles—then you can easily switch back and forth between sewing wovens and knits. However, I have noticed that sometimes when I sew knits and *don't* use ballpoint needles, the stitching formation can be irregular, or weird loops will show up. If that happens, always check your needle, because that is usually the source of the problem—and it's far easier to fix than messing around with delicate tension!

Make sure you change your needles every now and then. It is very important that they always be straight and sharp. If your machine starts acting odd or you notice skipped stitches, check your needle first—it could be chipped or bent.

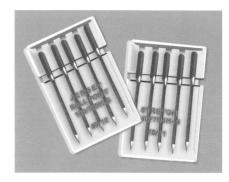

TIP

For 4-thread overlock machines, use the thread that matches the fabric in the left needle. That is the stitch that will show through if you pull at the seams.

THREAD

The vast variety of thread qualities and styles on the market can be totally daunting. For most serger sewing, you'll want to use a basic all-purpose **polyester cone thread** or **cotton/polyester thread**. Since the serger eats up a lot of thread, the cone style is the best: it has more thread, which will save you money and the hassle of changing spools, and it's cross-wound for fast unwinding. You can use regular tube or spool threads, but remember to use the spool caps to keep them from flying off the machine or getting their threads caught in the notch of the spool. Another thread to be aware of is a **textured nylon**, also called woolly nylon. It has a fluffy feel and more stretch than all-purpose threads, and is great for four-way stretch activewear like swimsuits or for decorative edging. **Decorative threads** come in polyester, nylon, and rayon with metallic, shiny, and variegated effects. You can customize the look of your garment by using these threads in the loopers of your machine and playing with the stitch length.

For most projects using a 3-thread overlock machine, you'll need three cones of the same color thread. This can get expensive, especially if you are making clothing in many different colors. It's easiest to buy groups of three same-color cones in a few basic colors like white, black, gray, red, and a pastel (green, blue, or pink). To economize even more, just buy two cones of the same colors (used for the loopers) and then buy a small spool that matches the fabric of your garment for the needle thread. If you turn the garment to the correct side and pull at the seams, the only threads you'll see are the needle threads. Those are the most important to match.

Getting By

For a conventional machine, 1 spool of matching all-purpose thread with a spool cover

Recommended

3 all-purpose cotton-wrapped polyester thread cones in black and white and 1 spool of thread that matches your fabric

Pro

3–4 cones of all-purpose cotton-wrapped polyester thread that match your fabric

STORAGE TIP

To keep thread from unwinding, use some cloth tape, like medical tape or tennis grip tape, or wrap a piece of paper around the cone. Store upright in a plastic box to protect from dirt.

TWEEZERS AND NEEDLE THREADERS

When you sew with a serger, you need to thread three or four parts—and these parts are in small, fairly difficult-to-reach places. I recommend buying a long pair of tweezers for threading the loopers; a regular needle threader is helpful, too. The latter usually comes with your serger when you buy it.

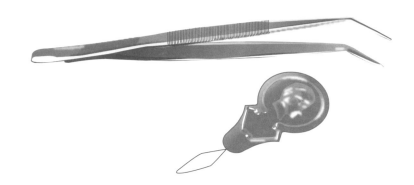

ROTARY CUTTER AND MAT

Because they're…well, stretchy, stretch fabrics tend to move around a bit during cutting. It's easier to cut them with a rotary cutter and a mat than with shears (though shears are always handy to have around for trimming).

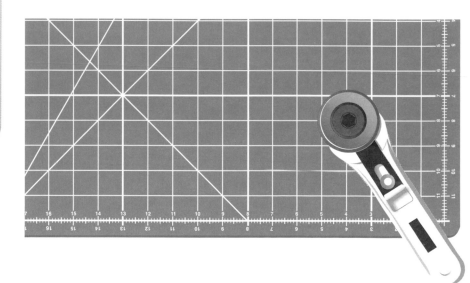

THE BIG TEN
ADDITIONAL SUPPLIES TO HAVE HANDY

Here are some other items that you'll find helpful when working on the projects in this book. For a comprehensive guide to using these, check out *Sew U*.

1. Shears (8"–10") for cutting fabric

2. Small embroidery scissors for clipping threads

3. Orange-handled paper scissors for cutting pattern paper and other pattern-making projects. Don't ruin your precious fabric shears by cutting paper. Just get paper scissors—they cost only a few bucks and are worth it!

4. Magic tape

5. 18" by 2" wide clear ruler

6. Pins

7. Weights (you can use substitutes like soup cans or other small heavy objects)

8. Tape measure

9. Pencil, pens (including a washable marking pen), erasers

10. Wide banner paper on a roll

CHAPTER 2
KNITS AND BOLTS

Getting to Know Stretch Fabrics

I'M A TACTILE PERSON—AND A TEXTILE PERSON. MY FAVORITE PART OF DESIGNING CLOTHING IS PLAYING WITH FABRIC.

I love spending hours lost in the aisles of a fabric store, poring through bolts and bins and picking out what sparks my interest, and then creating pieces based on the fabric. Some designers, however, work the opposite way: First they think of a shape they want to make, and then they choose a fabric that fits the garment's style. Whatever your preference, one thing is certain: If you're going to be working with stretch fabrics, you need to know how they act.

Fabrics are either woven or knitted. In my first book, *Sew U*, we focused on wovens, which are rigid fabrics formed by a horizontal yarn crossing over a vertical yarn. While some stretch fabrics are actually wovens made with stretch fibers, for the purposes of this book we are focusing on stretch fabrics that are knitted.

Knit fabrics are made with a flatbed or vertical machine (or occasionally by hand, with knitting needles). Yarns are looped repeatedly, interlocking to form the sheath of fabric. Because of this looping, the fabric is naturally going to be somewhat stretchy. Just how much depends on a number of factors. To familiarize yourself with the range of stretch fabrics, grab a variety of T-shirts and sweatshirts and pull them crosswise. They are all probably a bit different, but none is totally stiff.

PROPERTIES
OF STRETCH FABRICS

There are a few criteria that define different types of stretch fabrics—or, for our purposes, knits. It's essential to understand how these variables work, both for sewing and for the design of your garments.

Fiber

A fabric can be natural—wool, silk, or cotton—or man-made, like polyester, acrylic, or nylon. Each kind of fiber has its own feel, degree of warmth, and degree of slipperiness. Think of the thickness and warmth of a wool jersey dress versus a cotton jersey T-shirt. Think of how a nylon slip feels and functions differently because of its fabric.

Knitting Style

The style of knit used for a fabric will affect the way it stretches and the way it hangs. Is it a jersey, an interlock, or a rib? A ribbed tank top will cling to your body, making it fit very differently from a jersey tee, which will hang soft and loose. Interlocks will have a stiffer, thicker, less drapey quality.

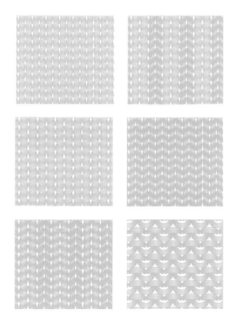

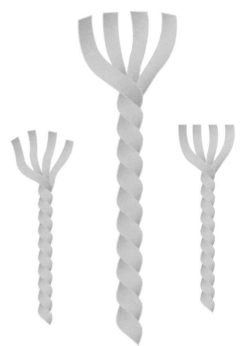

Thickness of Yarn

Some knits are very delicate and use only a single ply (strand) of yarn, while others are quite thick. Think of those fancy four-ply cashmere sweaters you covet in the winter, versus the delicate, layerable properties of a thin silk jersey undershirt.

Stretchability

Not only does the knitting style affect the degree of stretch, but the presence of stretch fibers such as spandex in a blend with either natural or man-made fibers has a huge impact on the fabric's behavior. You can feel the difference between something that has 2 percent spandex in it versus 5 percent spandex. Going to the fabric store and familiarizing yourself with both is a great way to get an idea of what you want. There are different types of stretch fabrics, including comfort stretch (with a touch of stretch to make street clothing and loungewear more flexible) and activewear stretch (athletic gear and the like, designed to be used and abused). Spandex and other stretch fibers also help with the recovery or "memory" of the fabric. Think of

cotton/spandex leggings: They hold your body in and don't sag. Cotton thermal long johns, on the other hand, sag in the butt and knees when you wear them for a long time.

Consider the function of the garment you'll be making when you decide on a fabric—and, while we're on the subject, when you decide to buy something in the store. My friend bought a knitted bikini by a very high-end designer and wore it swimming, and it stretched out so much that it almost fell off in the water! She tried to return it, and the salespeople were shocked that she would try to swim in it. My friend said, "But it's a *swim*suit!" but they insisted it was for fashion, not function.

You can test the stretchability of your fabric: Just cut a 10"-by- 4"-wide strip. If it can stretch to 15", then it has a 50 percent stretch; if it stretches to 20", then it has a 100 percent stretch, and so on.

Direction of Stretch

Most stretch fabrics have a two-way stretch, meaning that they stretch widthwise—like your favorite T-shirt, which expands side-to-side to accommodate your size. Some stretch fabrics have a four-way stretch and stretch in width *and* length. Those are mostly used in activewear like bathing suits and bike shorts, which need to stretch in all directions.

Confused? Don't be. There is an endless array of stretch fabrics out there, but I will touch on those that are most accessible and commonly used (these are also the kinds of fabrics I recommend for the patterns and styles in this book).

TYPES
OF STRETCH FABRICS

Stretch fabrics really run the gamut. There are basic T-shirt fabrics like cotton jersey, interlocks, and ribs. There are also versions made out of wool, silk, polyester, and nylon. There are versions with a pile (plush surface texture), like terry cloth. And there are very thick stretch fabrics, like polar fleece and loose sweater knits.

Jersey

Jersey is a great basic fabric. As a rule, it features a flat, plain knit on both the front and the back, and when you cut it, it will curl up a bit on the edges. Generally speaking, it has the least amount of stretch compared to other knits (unless, of course, it has spandex in it).

Wool jersey is great for fall and winter tops, skirts, and dresses because it combines warmth with comfort and flexibility. Buy a high-quality wool jersey, though, or it will be itchy. If that's the case, you can always line your garment with a thin nylon tricot (like the kind used for panties and slips).

Cotton jersey is great for tops, shorts, dresses, and leggings—and, of course, it's the classic T-shirt fabric. You might also want to look for blends with rayon in them, which have a slinkier, sexier, and softer feel. These are great for drapey tops and dresses but also give a nice twist to standard T-shirts.

Silk jersey is great for dressier, sexier tops and dresses. It's expensive but has a beautiful look and feel to it, and often boasts a subtle sheen. Silk jersey dyes well, so you can usually find it in a large assortment of colors and even prints, which are perfect for making Diane von Furstenberg–style wrap dresses. Silk jersey is also used for long underwear, which feels wonderful against the skin.

Interlock

An interlock knit is made from two interlocking yarns rather than one yarn. It's thicker, stiffer, and more resilient than jersey and is great for a variety of uses—although it's not usually ideal for drapey styles. Using an interlock knit for a tank dress or miniskirt is a good idea, because the fabric will be a bit more forgiving and less clingy than jersey, which tends to reveal every detail of the posterior region.

Ribs

A ribbed fabric is just what you think it is: It has long, usually vertical ribs in the fabric texture. These ribs expand when pulled, giving it more stretch and recovery than other fabrics. That is why ribbed fabric is often cut into strips and used for neck holes, waistbands, and cuffs. The classic rib style is a 1-by-1 rib, meaning there is one rib on the surface next to one rib underneath. You can also find 2-by-1 and 2-by-2 ribs (also called poor boy–style ribs). Because of their stretchy nature, ribbed fabrics cling closely to the body—they stick to your ribs! So when you're shopping for fabric for a particular style, keep this in mind. Most ribbed styles are sold in a variety of fibers. The classic T-shirt rib is usually a 1-by-1 cotton rib. But you can also find fabrics like a wool 2-by-2, for instance, which is great to make a winter turtleneck or to use as trim on a winter coat.

Fleeces

These fun, fuzzy fabrics come in a range of styles, from polar fleece to classic sweatpant fleece to French terry. I know that many sewers like using polar fleece because it's easy to find, warm, cheap, and easy to sew, but I'm not a big fan, for aesthetic reasons (it just reminds me a bit too much of blankets and mountaineer gear, I guess—cozy, but definitely not chic). I'm going to stick to recommending classic gym-class sweatshirt fleece for this book. You can get this at most stores. The hard part, though, is that you'll need to find a 1-by-1 rib for the cuffs and collar if you are making a sweatshirt, and if you go beyond basic black or white, it's hard to find a rib that precisely matches the color of your fleece. If you can't find a match, it can actually look cool if the trim color is slightly off, as in a medium gray-heather hoodie with pale gray cuffs—or you can use a contrasting cuff and neck color, like bright red, as a cute and unexpected design element.

Sweater Knits

You can find some great novelty knits out there. It can be fun to, say, find some metallic Lurex novelty jersey and just make a plain T-shirt out of it. I am not a huge sweater-knit fan, though, because it can be difficult to work with: Raw edges fray apart quickly, and hemming is hard without a cover-stitch machine.

Piqué

This fabric is often associated with the classic polo shirt. It doesn't have a lot of flexibility, but it is a solid knit that works great for shirts and dresses.

Terry Cloth

You can make more than beachwear with terry. Think of it like any other stretch fabric. The loops of the fabric help to hide lumps and bumps, unlike unforgiving jerseys and ribs. This makes it great for a modern cover-up or a fun summery dress.

Spandex Nylon

We usually just call this spandex, and we all know what it means: shiny leggings, bathing suits, and workout clothing. Unless you are a rock star, it's probably best saved for working out.

Wovens with Some Stretch

These are better for the projects in *Sew U*. They might be called stretch denim or stretch shirting; a normally woven, rigid fabric has a small percentage of spandex in the weave for a comfortable amount of stretch. They usually are treated and sewn like woven fabrics, not like knits. If a woven fabric has a lot of stretch in it, it may be possible to use it with a pattern made for knit fabrics. It's not really recommended, though.

BUYING AND HANDLING
STRETCH FABRICS

In your local fabric store, you are most likely to see a range of cotton jerseys and ribs in solid colors, some interlocks with baby-appropriate patterns, lots of polar fleece, regular sweatshirt fleece in some basic colors, and maybe a small selection of wool/poly blend jerseys. At higher-end fabric stores, you might find silk jerseys and some novelty knits. These fabrics are sold by the yard and rolled on tubes. The fabric will be either rolled open, so that the entire width of the fabric runs along the length of the tube, or folded in half and rolled on a bolt. Some knit fabrics are tubular. This means they're knitted in a ring rather than a flat sheet, so they don't have an edge (these are time-saving for the bodies of T-shirts). When considering buying these, keep in mind that if the fabric is, say, 30″ wide in tubular form, it is actually 60″ wide if you cut it open.

FINDING FLATTERING FABRICS

When you're shopping, it's easy to get excited by the fabrics you see. This isn't always a good thing! I remember finding some cotton jersey with little puppies printed all over it. I made a T-shirt out of it, then realized that I would never wear a T-shirt like that—ever! So I guess what I'm saying is, be careful not to buy fabrics just because they're cute or interesting. Instead, try to imagine the fabric in garment form. Many fabric stores have mirrors, so I suggest grabbing the bolt of fabric and holding it up against you and seeing how it drapes, how the color and pattern look, and whether it flatters you.

FINDING FABRICS THAT WORK WITH THE DESIGN AND YOUR FIGURE

Stretch fabrics tend to accentuate the body. Many stretch garment styles are form-fitting; even looser styles are often draped to emphasize the figure. With that in mind, if you are self-conscious about certain parts of your body and want to camouflage them, I would suggest buying darker colors and prints and avoiding designs that are super-clingy. However, in my years of designing, I've learned that there are many ways to use design elements and fabrics to accentuate whatever it is you want to show off. For instance, if you have wide shoulders and thick biceps, you can make a dress with narrow shoulders but give the sleeves a puff and a loose bell shape. This will create the illusion of slimmer shoulders, and the puff/bell shape will hide your arms. If you are less than enthused about your waist, try making a tight-fitting dress but in a print; this will deemphasize the specifics of your shape.

INVEST IN UNDERGARMENTS

Stretch fabrics, especially in snugger-fitting styles, don't keep any secrets. Unless you love the look of a butt-bisecting panty line under a tight-fitting miniskirt, it's best to buy—or make!—some skin-colored or neutral undergarments with smooth edges. There are plenty of seamless bras on the market that are made to be worn under T-shirts; I also like camisoles with built-in bras. I am also a big fan of skin-colored spandex slips. You never have to worry about whether your dress is slightly sheer if you wear a form-fitting slip under it.

The Six Commandments:
Super-Important Stretch Fabric Tips

1. ALWAYS BUY A LITTLE BIT OF EXTRA FABRIC. It helps with testing out the stitch length, width, and tensions of your machine. Besides, if you mess up, you won't have to run back to the fabric store. You can always use leftovers as a small element of another design.

2. CONSIDER YOUR DESIGN WHEN CHOOSING FABRIC. Do you really need a camisole top in wool jersey? Wouldn't it drape more nicely and feel better against the skin in a silk jersey?

3. PREWASH OR DRY-CLEAN FABRIC BEFORE CUTTING IT. Then you'll never have to worry that it will spring any surprises on you after it's sewn. Preshrinking is key!

4. WHEN YOU'RE FIDDLING AROUND WITH STRETCH FABRICS, THEY MIGHT ACTUALLY STRETCH. Let fabric relax for a few hours on the cutting table before you cut. If you cut a skirt while the fabric is stretched out, then your knee-length skirt might end up a miniskirt once the fabric has recovered. (And your miniskirt might look more like a bandeau bra.)

5. HANG ON TO YOUR SCRAPS. As you make more and more projects, attach a piece of the fabric to the pattern you used. That way, you'll always remember which kinds of fabric work best for each pattern.

6. STORE ALL YOUR STRETCH FABRICS TOGETHER; DON'T MIX THEM WITH WOVENS. It's easier to figure out what to make if you have organized your fabrics by types, such as stretch/knits, coatings, bottom-weights (denim and twills), lightweight wovens (for blouses and shirts), and so on.

CHAPTER 3
PATTERN RECOGNITION

How to Use Them, How to Change Them Up

PATTERNS ARE THE BUILDING BLOCKS OF EVERY GARMENT—AND THIS BOOK, JUST LIKE *SEW U*, COMES WITH SEVERAL BASIC ONES.

These patterns, and my instructions, are meant to help you learn some simple pattern-making skills so you can gain the confidence to alter your own store-bought patterns, invent your own designs, and remake clothes you already have. The skills you learn while working with these basic patterns can be applied to any patterns and clothing you have. Take a look at the various T-shirts you own. What makes them different? Sleeves are shorter or longer; necklines are scooped or V-shaped. You will start to notice that most T-shirts have the same basic shape and that through pattern-making you can use slight changes to make them all very different. It's kind of like cooking Tex-Mex: Tacos, burritos, and enchiladas use many of the same ingredients, just in different proportions and made into different shapes. Once you're familiar with how patterns work (the ingredients), don't be afraid to view them as a starting point for your own ideas—you'll definitely want to think outside the boundary lines!

One thing that's great about patterns for stretch fabrics is that they're easy. They usually don't have any darts or closures, like buttons and zippers. You'll really just be stitching the seams, finishing hems, and maybe adding some elastic. So when you look at these patterns, you'll notice that in comparison to woven patterns, they look very, very simple—and they are! Plus it's very easy to alter and mix and match all of these pieces. I'll give you plenty of ideas in this chapter and throughout the book.

BACK TO BASICS
PATTERNS IN THIS BOOK

These basic patterns can be mixed and matched to form a variety of looks. See the project chapters for more ideas for how to take them to another level.

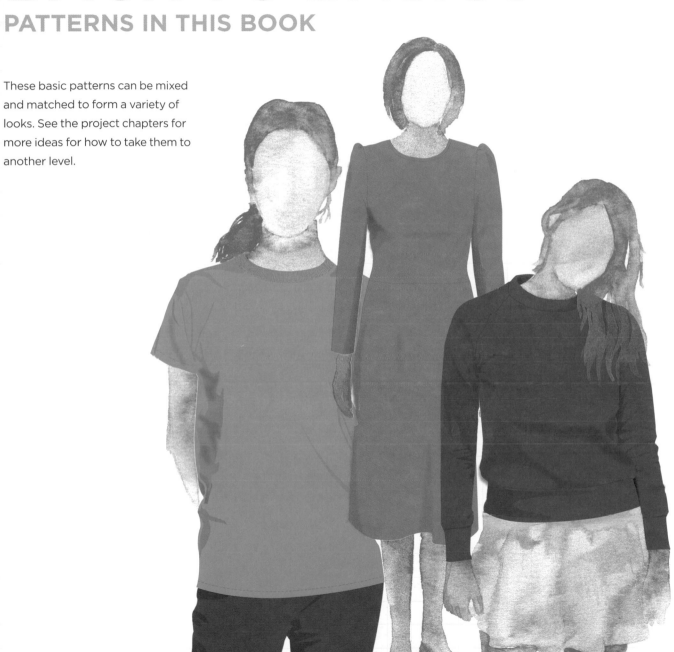

BASIC TEE

A slim-fit (not skintight) crewneck
T-shirt

1. Basic front
2. Basic back
3. Basic short sleeve
4. Neck rib

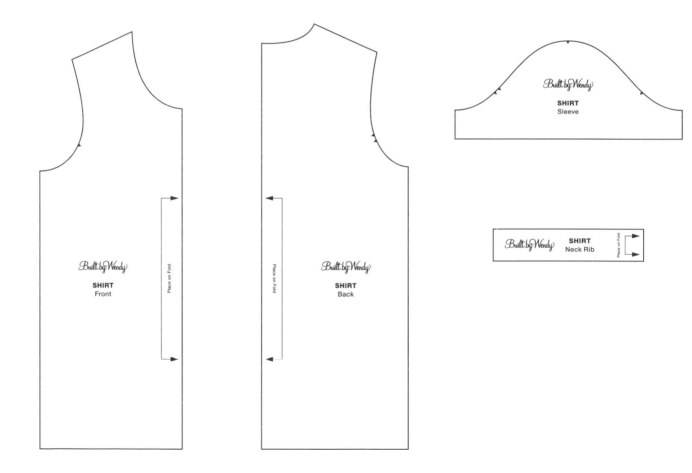

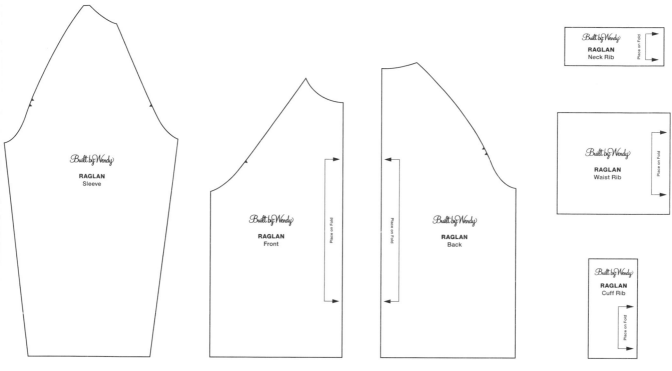

HOODED
RAGLAN TEE

A regular fit that can be used for
hoodies or T-shirts

1. Raglan front
2. Raglan back
3. Raglan long sleeve
4. Cuff rib
5. Hem rib
6. Neck rib
7. Hood

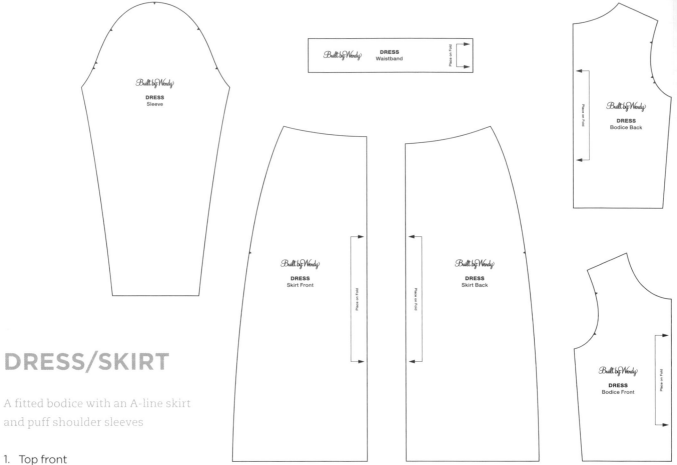

DRESS/SKIRT

A fitted bodice with an A-line skirt
and puff shoulder sleeves

1. Top front
2. Top back
3. Puff sleeve: long and short
versions
4. Skirt front: knee-length and mini
versions
5. Skirt back: knee-length and mini
versions
6. Waistband

Seam allowances for all patterns
are $1/4''$

The great thing about many stretch styles is that one size often fits many, if not all. The size you choose to make won't necessarily be the size that you usually wear. It all depends on the stretchability of the fabric and how snug you want your garment to be.

SIZE MATTERS

Measure Yourself

Then compare the measurement to the size chart below.

CREWNECK	XS		SMALL		MEDIUM		LARGE	
	BODY	GARMENT	BODY	GARMENT	BODY	GARMENT	BODY	GARMENT
CHEST	32"	34"	34"	36"	36"	38"	38"	40"
WAIST	25"		27"		29"		31"	
HIP	36"		38"		40"		42"	

RAGLAN	XS		SMALL		MEDIUM		LARGE	
	BODY	GARMENT	BODY	GARMENT	BODY	GARMENT	BODY	GARMENT
CHEST	32"	35½"	34"	37½"	36"	39½"	38"	41½"
WAIST	25"		27"		29"		31"	
HIP	36"		38"		40"		42"	

DRESS/SKIRT	XS		SMALL		MEDIUM		LARGE	
	BODY	GARMENT	BODY	GARMENT	BODY	GARMENT	BODY	GARMENT
CHEST	32"	34"	34"	34"	36"	36"	38"	38"
WAIST	25"	34"	27"	27"	29"	29"	31"	31"
HIP	36"	36"	38"	38"	40"	40"	42"	42"

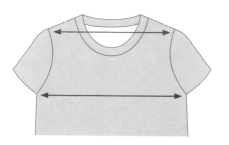

Measure Your Favorite-Fitting T-shirt

See the size chart to determine what size the actual garment will be, and cut out the size that best matches the size of your favorite tee. If you use this technique, however, make sure you buy fabric that has a similar stretchability. (You might want to take your favorite tee, and any other garments you love, to the fabric store for a side-by-side comparison.)

Consider Your Style

With knits, choosing different sizes can produce totally different looks. Fabric plays a part in this, too. For instance, if you're using the T-shirt pattern, a size small in a 1-by-1 rib will create a tight-fitting baby tee, while a size large in a slinky rayon-cotton jersey will result in a slouchy, loose look.

PATTERN-MAKING BASICS

There are many ways to go about designing. One way is to focus on an interesting fabric. Another is to add an interesting trim or technique to a basic pattern. The third way is to change the pattern into something different and possibly even more exciting. A good designer will use one or all of these to create a style—but will always keep in mind just how far to go. For instance, if you have a really interesting fabric with a large floral design, it might be a good idea to keep the pattern very simple and not use any trims. Likewise, if you have a very complicated pattern, like a dress with an asymmetrical gathered bust and ruffled hem, it might shine through better if you use a very plain fabric. Or you can use a very simple fabric and pattern, like a basic white jersey crewneck T-shirt, but choose a really cool piping to insert along the side seams, and make that the focus of the garment. In the same way you employ pattern-making techniques to alter basic patterns for wovens, you can use similar (but much easier!) methods to alter these patterns for knit fabrics. With these skills at hand, you can make even a basic T-shirt into something very special.

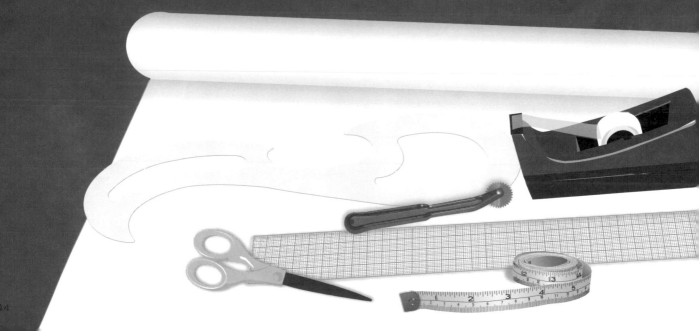

Supplies

These are things I use daily for most of my pattern-making.

Roll of banner paper (about 30"–50" wide). Or you can get by with regular 8 ½"-by-11" printer paper (you'll just need to tape some of it together).

Magic tape, used constantly to patch up all your patterns.

Paper scissors for cutting up all your patterns.

18" by 2" clear ruler. This is something I can't live without.

French curve for tracing your necklines and armholes (you can fudge it without this, but it's nice to have).

Cloth tape measure to measure your body against the specs of the pattern, among other uses.

Tracing wheel for transferring pattern lines to other paper.

Ch-ch-ch-ch-changes: Pattern-making Techniques

The most commonly used techniques for altering knit patterns are **adding**, **trimming**, **folding**, and **slashing/spreading**. These make your garments longer or shorter or wider or narrower—all over or in specific parts. Adding and trimming either add or remove width or length from your pattern *using the pattern edges*. So if you add or remove from a pattern shape that is narrower at the top than at the bottom, such as an A-line skirt, then the skirt hem will get either wider or narrower. Slashing and spreading, and folding, either add or remove mass from your pattern *within the pattern pieces*. So if you slash and spread (to expand) or fold (to contract) an A-line skirt, the hem width will stay the same, since you are adding or removing within the pattern. If you are slashing and spreading vertically, the hem width will change.

> **TIP**
>
> In most cases, if a skirt or dress is straight, then you can just add or trim. If the skirt or dress is A-line, then you can decide what method to use, depending on whether you want your hem narrower or wider (trim or add) or the same (slash or spread or fold).

Adding means using your ruler to add length or width to your pattern following the shape of the existing hem or seam you are adding to. Use this to add seam allowances as well.

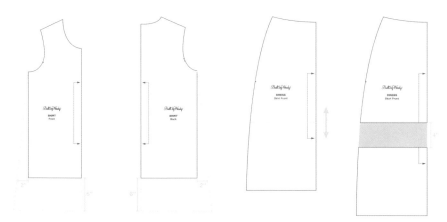

Trimming means cutting off part of your pattern that you don't want. You can use trimming for shaping purposes: For instance, if you want to have a deep scoop neck instead of a crew neck, just draw the shape of the neckline and cut it out. Done! You can also use trimming for shortening purposes, such as when the sleeves are too long. Draw a line for the new length and cut there. Don't forget to include the seam allowance or hem when necessary. You can also trim to make something slimmer. If the pattern is too wide for your design, slim a little off the side seam parallel to the existing edge.

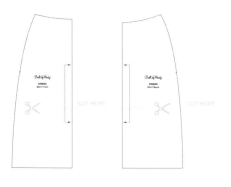

Folding is another way to shorten a pattern. It's the opposite of slashing and spreading, which I'll get to next. It's basically a form of trimming, except that you are removing from within the pattern rather than from the hem, in order to preserve the pattern's existing shape. If you want to shorten your T-shirt by 2″, you can just draw a horizontal line across the front and then draw another one parallel to it 2″ above the first line. Then fold the pattern so the two lines are together and tape the fold closed.

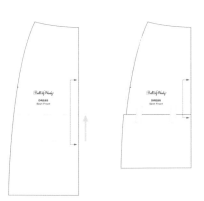

Slashing and spreading is used to add length or width to a garment and can be used for slightly expanding or lengthening a garment or drastically altering its size.

For instance, suppose you want to make your slim pencil skirt into a dirndl-style gathered skirt. Here's what you do:

1. MEASURE THE width of the front pattern piece. Let's say, for example, it's 12″.

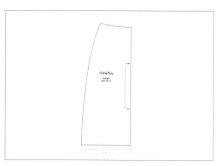

2. ON A LARGE piece of paper, draw one vertical line, and then another one 16″ away.

3. DRAW A HORIZONTAL LINE to connect the two vertical lines at right angles.

4. MAKE FOUR VERTICAL cuts evenly down the length of the front pattern piece.

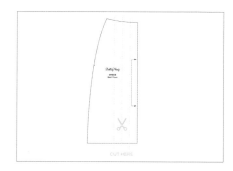

5. LAY THESE PIECES evenly within the 16″-wide box you created, with the pattern hem on the horizontal line.

6. TAPE THE PIECES down, trace the shape, label, and cut out.

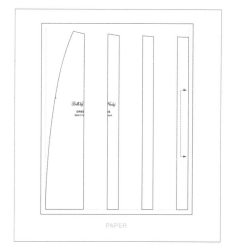

7. REPEAT THESE STEPS for the back piece.

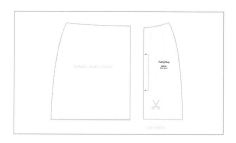

8. WHEN SEWING this skirt style, you'll gather front and back pieces into the waistband.

The same technique can be done with a T-shirt: You can take a snug tee pattern and make a loose blouse. First trim the neckline to the desired shape, then slash and spread to the desired width.

You can use slashing and spreading vertically on a pattern to add length.

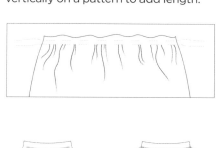

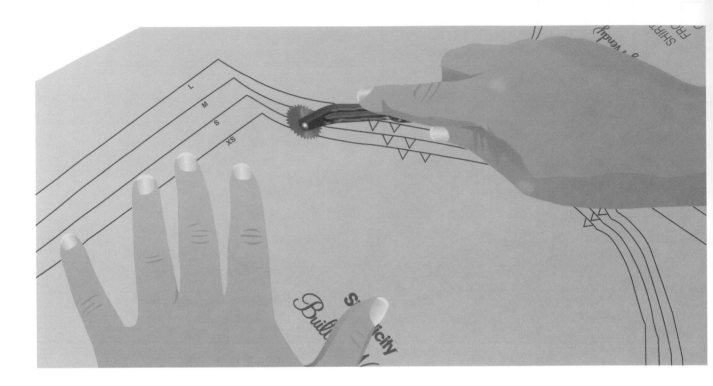

A Solid Idea: Transferring and Copying

If you plan on experimenting with the different sizes included in this book, which I recommend, you might want to trace the different-sized patterns onto banner paper instead of cutting out the tissue for just one size. Tissue is quite delicate, so it's nice to have a pattern on a sturdier paper—especially since these basic patterns are also the main templates for pattern-making. You'll be using them every time you make a new garment, so why risk rips? Just lay banner paper under your tissue (iron out the tissue first so it's smooth) and trace lines using your tracing wheel. Then outline the transferred perforations with a pencil, cut, and label each pattern piece with complete information.

If you have a basic T-shirt that fits well, you can easily make a pattern from it. The best way is to rip open the seams, lay pieces on paper, trace, and add seam allowances. But if you don't want to ruin your favorite tee, you can just lay the T-shirt flat and use your tracing wheel to outline the seams. The perforations will make an indentation on the paper but won't damage your shirt. Then you can trace with your pencil, add seam allowances, label, and cut. The best way to get a symmetrical pattern is to fold a piece of paper and lay half of the shirt on top. Before you cut, measure the shirt; afterward, measure the pattern and make any adjustments if you are off.

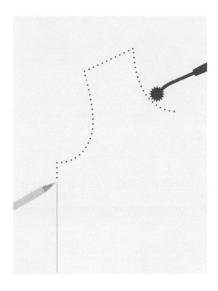

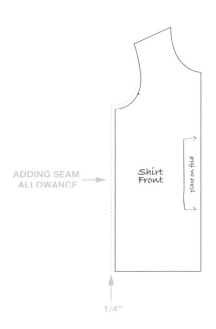

ADDING SEAM ALLOWANCE

Shirt Front

place on fold

1/4"

1. Fold paper in half, lay half of T-shirt on top, and run tracing wheel along seams.

2. Trace over perforated dots with a pencil.

3. Add seam allowances, label pattern, and cut out.

PICKING UP THE PIECES
HANDLING AND STORING PATTERNS

The most important thing to do once you have your patterns is to keep them organized. It's such a bummer to deal with a wadded-up, crinkled pattern that has some pieces missing—and it makes it almost impossible to actually sew anything! Once you open your commercial tissue patterns, either transfer them (by taping them to paper and cutting them out) or iron fusible interfacing on the back so they are more permanent. You can also transfer them to poster board. If you choose to leave them in tissue form—which is fine—just fold them nicely and either store them in the envelope or buy gallon-size zipper-close bags to put them in, along with the envelope, so you can identify the style easily.

You can do the same thing with patterns you make yourself using your banner paper. Just be sure to label the pieces. You can even make up a style number or name if you want. Say, for instance, that you've used a crewneck T-shirt pattern but made it into a scoopneck pattern instead. Just write on each pattern piece "Scoopneck T-shirt front" or "Scoopneck T-shirt sleeve" or "Style 001 Scoopneck T-shirt front." However you want to do it, just don't neglect to label all the pieces. I have forgotten to label pieces before, and trust me, you don't want to make the same mistake. For instance, I once found a sleeve shape with nothing marked on it, so I assumed it was garbage. Later I was looking at my raglan-sleeve sweatshirt pattern, and the sleeve was missing. It was such a pain to try to redraft a new sleeve pattern from scratch. Better to take two seconds to write the information down in the first place!

I also like to store all my stretch fabric patterns together and all my woven patterns together. Once you have a lot of patterns, it's helpful to subcategorize them, too: tops, dresses, skirts, and so on.

CHAPTER 4
BY THE SLICE

Preparation and Cutting

ONCE YOU'VE GOT THE TRICKY BUSINESS OF PREPARING YOUR PATTERN OUT OF THE WAY, YOU'RE READY TO CUT OUT THE FABRIC PIECES AND GET DOWN TO THE BUSINESS OF SEWING.

But wait, slow down! Once you cut into fabric, you can't take it back. That's why you need to perform the entire process, from preparing the fabric to laying out your pattern pieces, extremely carefully. In other words, as I reminded you in my first book, think twice, cut once! Whether you're cutting wovens or knits, you'll still want to follow the basic guidelines of cutting (which I cover in detail in *Sew U*), but some tips are important to keep in mind for knit fabrics in particular.

PREP TIME
HELPING YOUR FABRIC MAKE THE CUT

With knits—or any fabric—it's best to wash and dry the fabric first so you never have to worry about it again. It's annoying to have to take special care of your tees or to have them shrink into half-shirts after washing. So always shrink before cutting. Make sure the fabric is unwrinkled as well—even slight wrinkles can alter the fit slightly, and if you cut over a wrinkle, you will have a weird bump in your edge. Since it will be serged off, it's no big deal, but ideally you want to cut into smooth, flat fabric.

Knits have their own set of special precautions. Sometimes, I've noticed through the years, knit fabrics have areas of discoloration. You do not want to use those areas, for obvious reasons, so inspect the fabric carefully. Most knits are sold folded, whether they are open or tubular. But because of knit fabric's unique properties, there will be one or two seemingly permanent crease marks where the fabric is folded. Washing, drying, and ironing beforehand might get the creases out, but usually that doesn't work. I have definitely been guilty of

buying some tubular rib and simply laying my front and back pieces on those creases, only to find that my new shirt had a faded-out, unerasable crease down the center front and back! Don't be lazy. If the fabric is open (meaning it's folded with selvage edges), just refold it and cut along the edge to cut off the crease. If the fabric is tubular and you're not keeping the tube intact to make the body of something (none of my patterns are set up this way, so let's assume not), do the same thing to remove each crease.

HALF WIT
A WORD ABOUT FOLDING BEFORE CUTTING

Most knit fabric patterns work in halves, meaning you'll trace and cut the half-pattern shape on a fold and then open it up, to save time and create a symmetrical piece. If you have a large sheet of fabric, though, folding it right in the middle means that the leftovers might not be wide enough to be used. Instead, open your fabric up and then fold a quarter on each side into the middle, assuming that this amount of fabric covers your pattern. This is the best way to get the most folded fabric space.

DON'T

DO

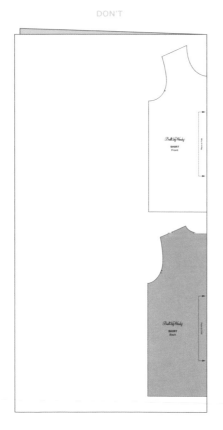

CREASE

FACE TIME
FINDING THE RIGHT SIDE OF THE FABRIC

Fabrics have two sides: the face, or right side, and the side that's called (sometimes with good reason) the wrong side. While they may look the same, they're often not. With printed or pile fabrics, it's easy to tell which side is the face, but other knits can be a bit harder to figure out. The face of jersey tends to be smoother than the wrong side and to curl up (curls roll toward the face). Interlocks tend to look identical on the right and wrong sides—the right side will be the side that faces out when you buy it. Ribs are a mixed bag: Sometimes you'll know right away which side is which (the looping in between ribs on the wrong side will somehow look kind of inside out), while with other ribs you won't be able to discern a difference. If you have trouble identifying the face, then don't worry about it. (And if you want to use the wrong side out as a design element, go for it—a fuzzy-fleece-out sweatshirt, for instance, can look really cool.) Just make sure that you sew all the pieces on the same side so your garment is uniform. It would be a bummer to catch your reflection in a certain light and notice that your right sleeve is slightly different from the rest of the garment!

RIGHT SIDE (FACE)

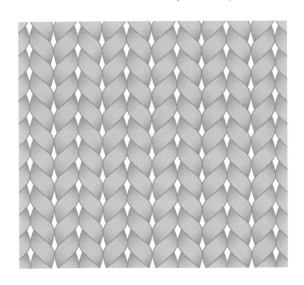

WRONG SIDE

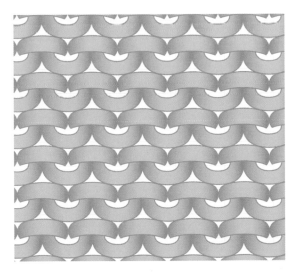

Like woven fabrics, knit fabrics have a direction, which you need to consider when cutting. This is easy to tell on printed fabrics where the design goes in one direction. But with knits, the real direction you need to consider is the stretch. Most fabrics are two-way stretch, meaning that they stretch width-wise. Some knits will stretch in the length or in all four directions: up, down, left, and right. Always double-check the direction of the stretch before you cut. You don't want to cut a super-snug T-shirt sideways so that it stretches on the up-down axis, because you won't be able to get it on!

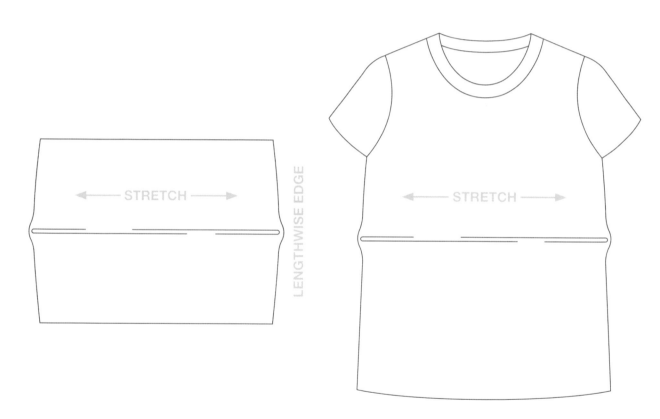

LENGTHWISE EDGE

STRETCH

STRETCH

HEADING IN THE
RIGHT DIRECTION

MATCHING
PLAIDS, STRIPES, AND PATTERNS

Since most knit patterns have only side seams to worry about (as opposed to things like button fronts and center back seams with zippers), it's best to line up the pattern pieces along the same horizontal plane. I generally use the side seam hem corner as the starting point and then make sure that the front and back patterns are lined up on that same point.

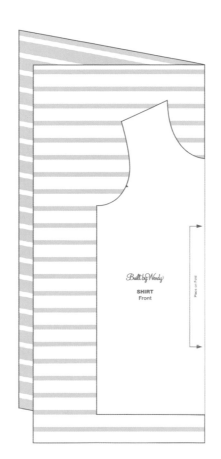

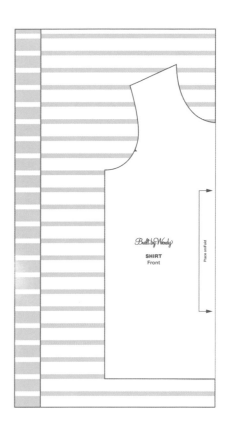

HOLDING IT DOWN
SECURING PATTERN PIECES ON FABRIC FOR CUTTING

There are two different ways to keep your pattern pieces in place for the cutting process: weights and pins. If you choose to pin your tissue-paper pattern to the fabric, I strongly suggest using **ballpoint straight pins**. They are usually easier than other pins to pin through knit fabric, and they also lessen the likelihood of fabric damage. Insert pins parallel to the pattern edge within the seam allowance area—this is important! In case you accidentally poke a permanent hole, that hole will be hidden within the seam. If you are using a pattern that has been transferred onto poster board, then pinning will be tricky. Instead, hold the pattern down with weights (anything from soup cans to metal washers will work) and use tailor's chalk or wax or a marking pen to trace the outline of the pattern onto the fabric. Then cut along the line.

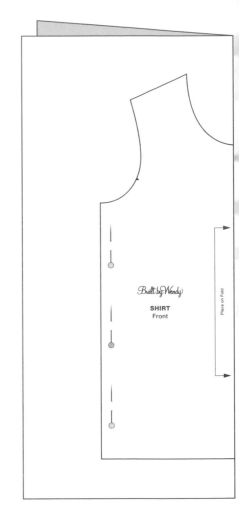

Staying Sharp: Shears and Cutters

There is nothing more frustrating than cutting fabric with dull shears. It's a good idea to write FABRIC ONLY on the handle of your favorite shears with a Sharpie so your roommate doesn't start using them to cut up flyers for her band's show. Since stretch fabric is stretchy and can move around a bit even when pinned or with weights, I suggest investing in a **rotary cutter** and

mat. It's just so much easier and more fun to cruise around the edges of your pattern cutting fabric effortlessly, as if it were pizza or cookie dough. Plus it's better for your wrist. Also, because the seam allowances for knits are usually $\frac{1}{4}$" to $\frac{3}{8}$", you want to be as precise as possible. Be sure to hold one hand down on the pattern when you cut this way.

One of the great things about sewing knits with a serger is that it beautifully trims your raw edge while finishing it. So if you do cut your edges unevenly, you can always smooth them out while serging.

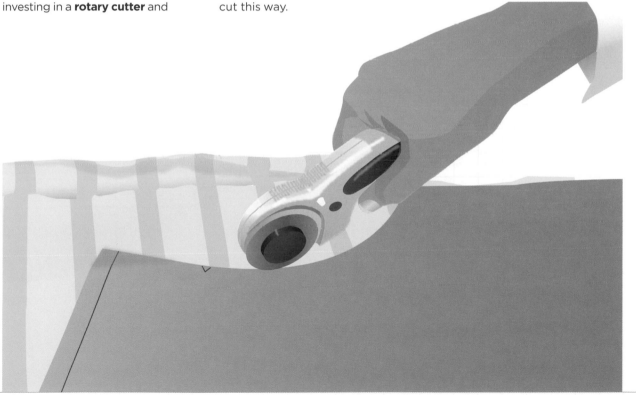

On Your Mark

Once you have cut out your pattern pieces, you're still not quite finished: You'll need to mark specific things like pocket placement and notches, which are matched up during sewing to ensure that the pieces are correctly aligned (each pattern will have its own specifics). When marking woven fabrics, it's easy to slice a notch or use an awl to make a punch hole. But because of the nature of knits, you must be extra-careful. If you do make a notch in the seam allowance, it must be very, very shallow, since your seam allowance is a narrow $3/8''$. Just use the very tip of your scissors (I recommend small specialty scissors) and go in only $1/8''$, or else the notch will show up on your finished garment as a horizontal slit on your side seam. For marking pocket placement or any other marking within the pattern, I suggest you use a washable marking pen to make a tiny dot rather than using an awl to make a punch hole, because the fabric will stretch a lot when the awl pushes through it.

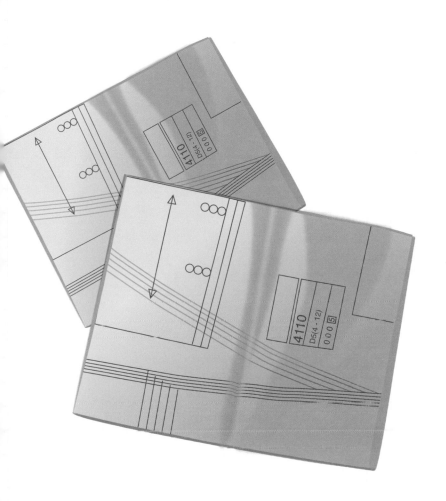

More often than not, I don't have time to sew my pattern pieces together immediately after cutting them. It's important, therefore, to store them carefully. The last thing you want is for a meticulously cut sleeve to slip beneath your desk and collect dust bunnies, so you have to recut it later. It's easiest to lay all the pieces in a pile (be sure that each one is laid fabric-face up) and roll them up like a tamale (back to my Tex-Mex analogies!). Stick the bundle in a clear plastic bag with all the trims and slip a piece of paper inside with a quick sketch or description of the garment for future reference. Or just tie the bundle together with a ribbon. Either way, it'll all be kept together neatly and securely.

BUNDLING

CHAPTER 5
A STITCH IN TIME

Quick Tips for Sewing Knits

MANY BEGINNING SEWERS DON'T EVEN KNOW WHAT A SERGER IS. WHEN I WAS STARTING OUT, I SURE DIDN'T.

I grew up learning on my mom's Bernina conventional machine. I would take her scraps of fabric and test out each kind of stitch with a turn of the dial. Back then I loved the way the zigzag stitch looked, and I'd often mess around with the stitch length and width. I would even sew on paper, making different designs using colored thread. It wasn't until I was curious about sewing knit fabrics that I realized the real purpose of zigzag stitching: it is a stretchable stitch, perfect for sewing knits. But as I looked at my T-shirts and wondered how I could alter them or make my own, I noticed that the seams inside my favorite tee didn't resemble my much-loved zigzag. Confused, I went to my local sewing machine/vacuum shop (I love it that those two are always thrown together!), where for the first time I saw a serger. What was that scary, crazy machine with four spools of thread perched on it? It looked quite intimidating, especially as I perused the instruction manual to see the overwhelming array of stitches and variables used for sewing knit fabrics. I just wanted to sew a T-shirt. Did I really need to know about all this stuff?

I remember that feeling all too well, and since it's probably how you're feeling, too, this chapter scales down the information to cover only what you need to know. It will show you the basic and specific skills you need to sew stretch fabrics—the kinds of stitches that will allow you to crank out a cute T-shirt minidress to wear out the same night. Unless you're an experienced sewer of knits, I recommend reading this chapter carefully *before* you attempt to make a project and consulting it regularly once you start sewing.

If you've never so much as sewed a stitch of any fabric in your life, I strongly encourage you to read and refer to *Sew U*, which has more hand-holding help for greenhorns. Advanced sewers, take note: If you are looking for instructions to make a complicated patchwork vest with decorative threading, you won't find them here. These are basic techniques, tried and tested through years of designing my collections, to help get your creative juices flowing.

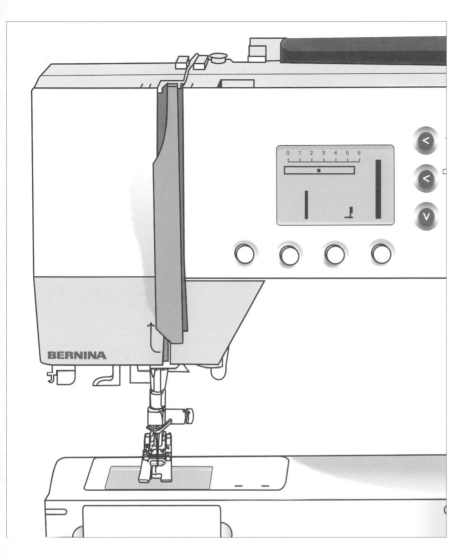

Now that you've gotten to know the basics of fabrics, patterns, and cutting for knits, you are ready to learn how to sew them. But before you can sit down and press that pedal, you need to understand the properties of the serger—a unique and temperamental machine that requires a bit of fiddling before you get the hang of it. For those who don't have one, I also give alternative instructions, so you can make the projects in this book using your conventional machine's handy zigzag stitch.

EQUIPPED FOR SUCCESS
FAMILIARIZING YOURSELF WITH YOUR MACHINE

SERGER

As discussed in chapter 1, the serger is the best machine for sewing stretch fabrics. It uses a combination of two, three, or four threads inserted into the needles and loopers to make an overlock stitch, which is why it is sometimes called an overlock machine. This stitch stretches while both joining and finishing the edges of fabric. When used on woven fabric, it will not stretch, but it will sew seams and finish them. Each brand of serger is slightly different in terms of where the dials are and how many stitches and variations it can do. When I first got my serger, I was completely overwhelmed by all the stitches I had to choose from. Then, when I was reading the manual, I came across the section about decorative stitching, and my head started to spin. It was all a bit too much—and I had been sewing for twelve years at that point! Sometimes in sewing, having too many options can be a bad thing, especially when you haven't mastered the basics. Each machine performs variety of stitches, so I'll cut through the fluff and focus on the ones I use and the ones that are useful for the projects in this book. If you're a skilled sewer and want to take it up a notch, your machine's manual will go into detail about all the stitches it can do.

Sergers feel very different to use from conventional sewing machines. Before you get down to business, practice using yours with some scrap fabric. The last thing you want to do is ruin your fabulous new fine-silk-jersey dress on the day of the party!

The stitches made by sergers encompass quite a few factors; the number of threads and stitch width are the main variables.

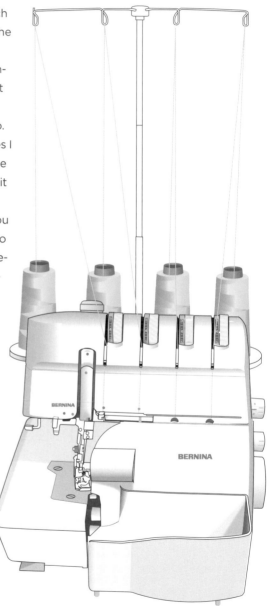

Spool Ties: A Few Useful Threading Tips

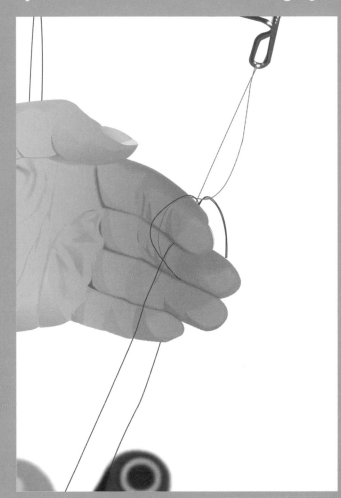

All you need to do is look at a serger to understand why threading one can be a bit complicated. You should read your individual manual for specific threading instructions, but here are a couple of techniques that I find helpful.

COLOR CODING

Color coding your threads helps to define which thread corresponds to which part of the stitch. Do this by using a different color thread for each needle and looper. I like to do it when I set up my machine for a project so that I can adjust the tension, width, and length of my stitch for the perfect balance.

TYING ON

This is a quick method to use when you need to change your thread color. Just clip thread at the cone, change cones, and tie the new thread onto the old thread and pull it through. When you "tie on," you will be creating a tiny knot, which needs to be pulled through the entire threading sequence of your machine. Since your thread runs through your delicate tension dials, it's best to pull it out of the tension dials and then floss it back in after the knot. Imagine if your dental floss had a knot in it: You wouldn't enjoy pulling that knot between your teeth! After pulling the thread through, you will reach the needle. Clip the knot off before you get to the eye of the needle, then thread the new thread through.

Stitches

Sergers perform three different types of stitches: overlock, roll hem, and flatlock. You can vary each of these by altering the number of threads used and the stitch width (sergers sew a complicated two-dimensional pattern, not a straight line of stitches). The stitch width depends on whether you are using the left or right needle and also on the cutting width setting you choose.

Overlock stitch is used for sewing seams and finishing edges.

• **4-thread overlock** uses both the left and right needles and both loopers. It is a strong, durable stitch sometimes called a 3-thread overlock with a safety stitch. It doesn't stretch as much as a 3-thread, so it's commonly used with heavier fabrics and wovens. Depending on the cutting width, it is usually 5–7mm (about ¼") wide.

• **3-thread overlock** is the most versatile stitch. I recommend this one for sewing seams in most of the projects in this book. It uses only one needle (your choice). With some slight adjustments, it can become a 3-thread roll hem and a 3-thread flatlock (more about those in a minute). If you use the left needle, the seam will be wider; the right needle will yield a narrower seam. Also, seam width depends on the cutting width and how heavy the fabric is. The wide setting (5–7mm; about ¼" wide) is what I suggest for all your basic serging. The narrow setting (3–5mm; a little less than ¼" wide) is good for lightweight fabrics and low-stress seams.

4-THREAD OVERLOCK

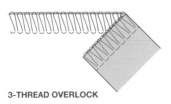

3-THREAD OVERLOCK

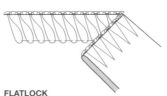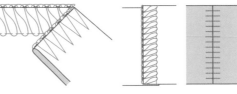

FLATLOCK

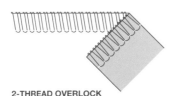

2-THREAD OVERLOCK

ROLL HEM

- **2-thread wrapped overlock** can be used for finished edges on seam allowances and decorative edging. There are a few reasons you may want to use this stitch. It is double-sided, meaning the stitch looks the same on the front and the back, which makes it great as a decorative seam. It also uses less thread, which is why it's great for expensive decorative threads, since you need only two spools. This is a great stitch to use if you make a wool blanket and finish the edges with some decorative yarn, for instance. We won't be using this stitch for the projects in this book, but it's still helpful to know what it is.

Roll hem stitch is used to finish open edges such as necklines and bottom hems. To use this stitch, you have to push a little lever so that a metal pin sticks out under the stitch plate. During sewing, the fabric edge curls slightly around this metal pin, and the stitches are wrapped around it. This is a very narrow stitch (about 1–3mm wide, or between 1/16″ and 1/8″ wide). For the projects in this book, we won't be using this stitch. If you really want to try it, I recommend using it to finish a raw edge of a hem instead of folding the edge back and topstitching it.

- **2-thread roll hem** is used for edging on lightweight knits. I don't use

this that often, because you have to add an upper looper converter on your machine. Sound complicated? It is, kind of—beginners are wise to avoid it altogether.

- **3-thread roll hem** can be used for edging but also as a very narrow seam to sew lace or lingerie or any other very fine knits. I love this stitch because it's very easy to switch to while using a 3-thread overlock. All you have to do is hit the roll hem lever.

Flatlock stitch is basically what it sounds like: flat. It is the same as overlocking in that two layers of fabric are stitched together, except that after you sew the seam, you grab each side of the fabric and pull, so that the two pieces of fabric, instead of "kissing," fall on top of each other. The way to do this is by loosening the tension of all your threads so that when you pull, the threads pull away from the seam, leaving room for the seam allowances to fall flat. It basically folds the seam allowance to the side, so it's good if you are sewing a tight-fitting garment and you don't want the bulk of a seam allowance inside. The bad part—or good part, depending on what you're trying to do—is that a flatlock seam is visible on the outside of the garment. So don't use it if you want your seams hidden. It is, however, a great seam if

you do want to show off your stitching as part of the design. You can even try using decorative or contrast-color threads to play it up.

For the projects in this book, we won't really need this stitch, but just assume that wherever there is overlocking, you can use a flatlock instead if you choose. You might have seen the flatlock stitch on gym sweatshirts or '70s-style T-shirts.

- **2-thread flatlock** is something I don't use that often, just because I don't feel like clipping threads and using the machine attachment that allows you to sew with only two threads.

- **3-thread flatlock** is the classic way to do a flatlock seam.

Stitch Variables

Several adjustments work hand in hand to ensure a flat and balanced stitch. Your serger manual should offer plenty of machine-specific instructions.

Stitch length is commonly set to 2.5mm. For heavier, thicker fabrics, use a larger stitch length (and looser tension), and for thinner fabrics use a tighter stitch length (and tighter tension).

Stitch width is determined by the needle position and cutting width setting. If you use the left needle, then the stitch can be 5–7mm wide (about 1/4" wide), while a right needle position will form a narrower 3–5mm-wide (about 1/8" wide) stitch. The cutting width you choose will depend on the heaviness of the fabric. For a very delicate fabric, you should use a smaller cutting width, while something like thick denim is better suited for a wider setting. If the seam is **cupping** (meaning it doesn't lie flat), then the cutting width needs to be smaller. This happens when the machine is trimming the fabric too wide and wrapping it in a too-narrow thread channel. Imagine squeezing a 9" piece of paper into an 8"-wide envelope and you'll get the idea. At the other extreme, if the loops are hanging off the fabric edge (which will make for a weak seam), then the cutting width needs to be bigger. (This is like putting a notecard into a letter-sized envelope—there's extra room.) You need to find a delicate balance between the cutting width and tension to get a perfect seam. Try a few test runs with your fabric before you start sewing.

STITCH WIDTH
NARROW

STITCH WIDTH
WIDE

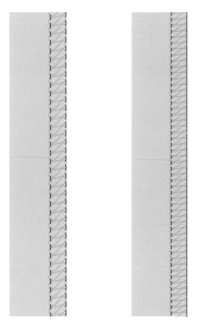

STITCH LENGTH
LOOSE

STITCH LENGTH
TIGHT

Thread tension needs to be adjusted depending on the stitch width and the bulkiness of the thread and fabric. Some machines are easy to adjust, while others tend to provoke…well, rage against the machine. If you're having tension issues, testing things out with different-colored threads is the quickest way to determine where the imbalance is. The most common symptom of an imbalanced stitch is when the looper thread is not meeting evenly at the cut edge. Check your serger manual for specifics on how to adjust everything.

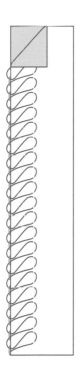

Differential Feed

A serger has two feed dogs, which work independently. You can adjust the setting of these feed dogs to prevent your fabric from gathering, puckering, and waving. Most of the time this setting should be on N, which is normal. You can also set the feed to deliberately gather or stretch the fabric as it's sewn for a puckering effect. This is used if you wanted to gather up a ruffle or stretch a neck rib to fit into a neck hole. I always find, though, that it's easier to do it by hand than to use the differential feed, since it takes a few practices to get it set correctly. Again, consult your machine's manual to get specific instructions, and beware if you're a total beginner.

Presser Foot Pressure

This should usually be set to normal, but lighter fabrics will work best with low pressure, and heavy and stiff fabrics should get the high-pressure setting.

NO, SERGE!
USING CONVENTIONAL MACHINES

Many of us don't have or can't afford a serger. And, as I emphasized in chapter 1, if you've never worked with knits before, you might not be ready to invest in one. But don't fret: You can still sew knits using your conventional machine. Many machines offer either a **mock overlock stitch** or, at the very least, a **zigzag stitch**. Because you don't have the trimming function that a serger offers, make sure that you cut out your patterns smoothly. Another key pointer: Conventional presser feet, because they press down so firmly, tend to get stuck and make knit fabrics stretch out, throwing off the sewing process. When I work with knits, I like to use a **walking foot**—a special presser foot that moves a little with the fabric—to prevent this problem. (Your sewing-equipment store will carry walking feet.) Your machine's manual will explain precisely how to adjust your tensions and presser foot so your knits don't stretch out and get wavy. As with a serger, or with any fabric and any kind of machine, always do a test run using your fabric to see how it behaves. You must get all your settings right, or you might ruin the garment pieces you've spent all that time prepping and cutting!

Even if you do use a serger to sew knits, you might use your conventional machine alongside it when sewing regular hems and topstitching if you don't have a cover-stitch/chain-stitch machine.

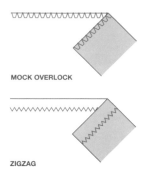

MOCK OVERLOCK

ZIGZAG

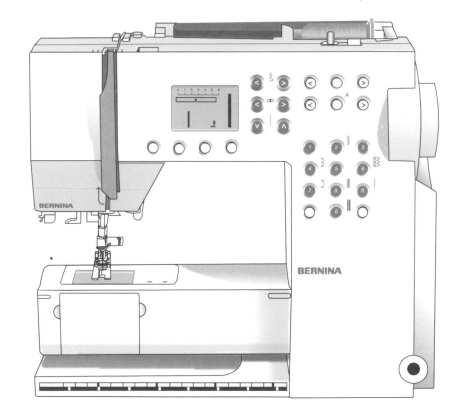

The Cover-Stitch/ Chain-Stitch Machine

This machine, while not necessary, is useful for its cover-stitch function, which is great for sewing hems on stretch fabrics. As discussed in chapter 1, it creates a double row of topstitching on top and a neatly serged seam underneath. Depending on your garment's style, you can create a narrow or wide cover stitch or one that has three rows of topstitching for a sportier look. The chain-stitch function is used more for wovens or for decorative purposes, but since it doesn't stretch much, it isn't really useful for the projects in this book.

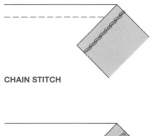

CHAIN STITCH

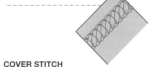

COVER STITCH

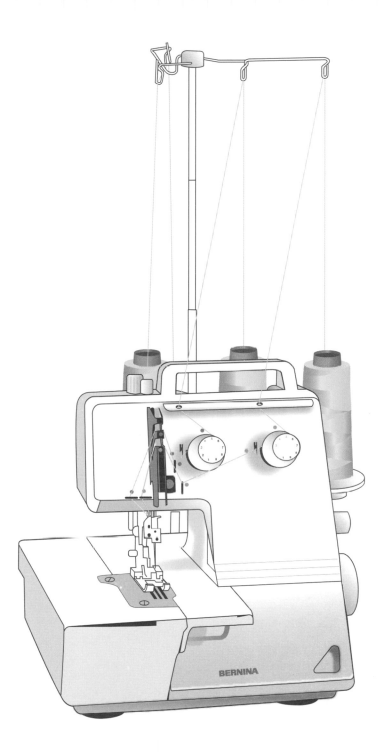

When I think about making a garment, it helps me to mentally divide the sewing process into two categories: sewing seams—attaching pattern pieces together to construct the garment—and finishing seams, which means hemming, binding, decorative stitching, facing, and lining, or any technique that eliminates raw edges from the garment at any openings (the sleeve, the bottom opening, the neck hole, and so on). With knit fabrics, this dichotomy is useful in determining which equipment to use. The best way to sew seams is with a serger, while the best way to finish seams is with a cover-stitch machine. I will present alternatives for conventional machine users and non-cover-stitch-machine users.

SEWING KNITS
A CRASH COURSE

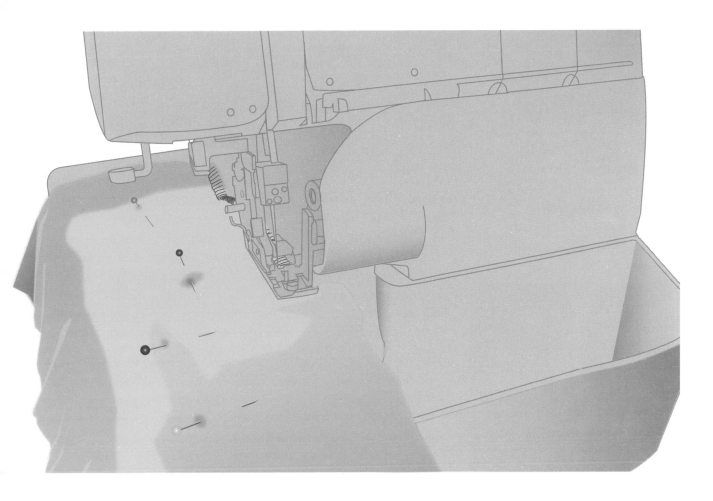

Sew Happy Together: Pinning Fabric Pieces

Before you sew two fabric pieces together, you might want to pin them in place so they don't slip around (especially if you're a beginner). This is a particularly useful technique for knits because of their stretchiness. Pin the pieces face to face, and place pins about 1″ from the fabric edge so the

serger's knife doesn't cut into a pin—ouch! Unlike with wovens, this is not within the seam allowance, because knits have a smaller seam allowance. Place the pins either parallel or perpendicular to the edge, as many or as few as you're comfortable with, and remove them as you sew. I usually don't use pins because I'm so accustomed to sewing, especially on small seams such as shoulders, but

most novice sewers like to use them for insurance. Just don't use them on super-delicate knits, because you run the risk of damaging the fabric (test the pins on a scrap first if you're not sure). Once you get used to your machine, you can just hold the fabric together with your fingers as you feed it in.

Seams

When you're ready to sew a seam, just place your fabric at the front of the presser foot and gently press the pedal, and the feed dogs will pull your fabric under and start sewing it. Here's the thing about a serger: it cranks out stitches loud and fast. Don't be scared; once you get the feel of your machine, you will be cruising along.

CHAIN, CHAIN, CHAIN: DEALING WITH SERGER THREAD TAILS

Unlike conventional machines, the serger keeps sewing whether or not there is fabric underneath. With a serger, instead of starting on the fabric, as you would with a conventional machine, you will start sewing *before* the needle meets the fabric and continue after you're done, leaving a chain of thread at both the beginning and the end of the seam. (If you did this on your conventional machine, your needle thread would wrap around your bobbin and possibly break your needle. You would have to rethread the whole thing—a total nightmare!)

When you start your first seam, you'll want to take that few inches of thread chain at the beginning and sew it back into the seam. To do this, just grab the chain as you are sewing and pull it back around so the presser foot swallows it into the new stitching being sewn. This is called **sewing in the thread chain** or **oversewing the thread tail**. When you are finished sewing a seam, just keep sewing so you have a few inches of chain. At that point you can take your scissors and cut the chain. Then secure the thread chain by threading the chain through a large-eyed darning needle and slipping the needle into your seam, inside the overlock stitch. Usually, though, you don't have to do that, because it's not that often you have an open-end seam. The loose thread tail is usually secured by either hemming or attaching another piece (like a neck rib). If it is not secured, then you should either perform this procedure and then apply Fray Check (a special sealant used in sewing) to the end, or tie the chain in a knot.

> ### TIP
>
> The best and fastest way to serge is not to stop. Because the thread chain keeps going, you can sew most of the garment while laying on the pedal. Seriously! For instance, if you lay your T-shirt pieces face to face, you can serge one shoulder and then cruise past the neckline and pick up the other shoulder. Keep generating the thread chain until you have enough to turn your garment around or over, and start another seam. You can always trim and sew in the chain, no matter how long it is, and you'll save time and fussing.

SEAM ALLOWANCES

With conventional machines, the seam allowance—the extra bit of fabric built into the pattern piece—needs to be trimmed and finished once you sew the seam. The great thing about sergers is that seam allowances are trimmed and finished in one fell swoop. Most of the seam allowances on the patterns for knits are $1/4"$ to $3/8"$ wide. If you line up your raw edge of fabric at the edge of the foot, you will not be trimming off any fabric. Depending on which needle you use in your machine (the left needle will make a $1/4"$-wide stitch, while the right needle will make about an $1/8"$-wide stitch), the seam allowance you sew will be $1/8"$ to $1/4"$ wide. If the seam allowance on your pattern is wider—say $3/8"$, like the patterns in this book—then you have to line up your raw fabric along the seam allowance cutting guide on the front of the machine. If you line up the fabric at the $3/8"$ guideline, then the knife will trim off $1/8"$ of fabric while sewing a $1/4"$-wide seam.

With a conventional machine, you won't need to worry about cutting off extra fabric, but you should still make sure you don't stitch farther in than the pattern's seam allowance. When sewing on this machine, use a zigzag stitch or a mock overlock, if your machine offers that. Since knits don't unravel, there is no need to finish the seam, though it won't look very professional.

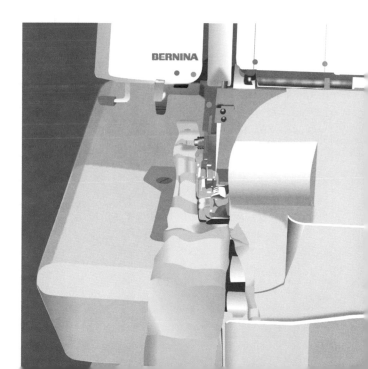

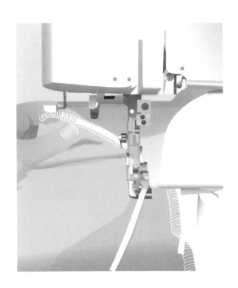

STABILIZING SEAMS WITH TAPE

If you look inside your T-shirts, you'll see that some of them have tape sewn into the shoulder seams. Stabilizing tape is available at any fabric store and is an important step for areas that you want to keep from stretching out (shoulders are the most common, but you might also want to use it inside pocket edges). Most standard serger presser feet have a slot in which to insert tape so the overlock stitch nicely covers the tape as you sew.

GATHERING

This technique—used for puff sleeves, ruffled hems, and the bottom part of Empire-waist dresses, among other things—can be performed with your serger using a 4-thread overlock stitch with the differential feed set at 2. Use long stitches: about 3–4 length. Sew one layer of fabric and watch it gather up a bit. Then pull the needle threads on your stitching, and it will gather up even more. Then, when you join it to another piece, its gathered quality will be made permanent.

I find that while you are overlocking, it can be a pain to switch over and start messing around with the differential feed just to do gathering. I prefer the old-fashioned way on a conventional machine. Here's a little refresher course on gathering:

1. Set your straight stitch to the longest stitch.

2. Stitch ¼" parallel to the raw edge; stitch another line ¼" below.

3. Grab the threads on each end of your line of stitching—make sure to grab the under threads (that is, the bobbin threads)—and pull. When you do this, the fabric will bunch up and gather. Use your fingers to push the gathering evenly to spread the ruffles closer or farther apart.

2

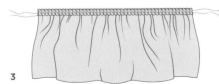

3

SEWING CURVES AND CORNERS

This is more difficult with a serger than with a conventional machine, where you can leave the needle in the fabric, lift the presser foot, and turn the fabric. There is no stop-and-turn function on a serger, because multiple threads are working continuously. Instead, you have to manipulate and stretch the fabric as you sew. When sewing a corner, it's easiest just to serge one side entirely to the end, let the thread chain continue, turn the fabric, and serge the other side. As you sew a curved seam, stretch the fabric with your hands so it forms a straight vertical line during the process. If you're a beginner—or if you're simply scared—practice, practice, practice doing this before you try to make something special with pricey fine jersey!

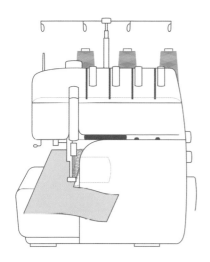
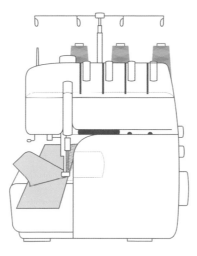

Finishing Edges

There are a variety of ways to finish raw edges, depending on the style of the garment and the kind of machinery you have.

ROLL HEM

The easiest way to finish an edge with a serger is to serge it. An overlock stitch will seal the hem, but it doesn't look particularly polished (though you may not be interested in a polished look if you're making a sweatshirt or a super-sporty tee). A much nicer option is the roll hem function on your serger, which is an easy, bulk-free way to finish an edge tastefully. It's especially nice on light or sheer fabrics. You can also use a decorative or contrast thread to jazz it up a bit.

HEMMING

The nicest way to do this is with a cover stitch from a cover-stitch/chain-stitch machine, as discussed, but you can create a mock version using a serger or a conventional machine.

1. Overlock the raw edge using either your serger or the mock overlock stitch on your conventional machine.

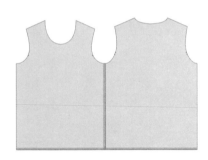

2. Fold back the hem at the desired height; pin and press for easier handling.

3. Topstitch using a narrow zigzag stitch. If the garment you are making isn't tight, you can use a nonstretchy straight stitch to topstitch; this works on, say, a loose skirt hem, since you won't be squeezing into it and thus stretching it out. Definitely use a zigzag on a tight T-shirt hem, since you will need to stretch the hem when pulling the shirt on and off. Each project in the book has specific instructions about this, but it's important to know the difference when you're designing your own garments.

4. You can also create a regular clean-finish hem, as you would for woven fabrics, where you just fold the hem over twice, sandwiching the raw edge into the fold. Once this is done, simply topstitch (either straight or zigzag, depending on whether the hem needs to stretch).

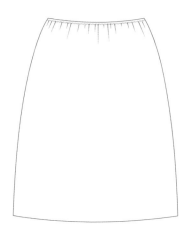

ELASTIC

You can finish an edge—like the waist of a skirt or the hem of a sleeve—using elastic; usually, $1/4$"- to $3/8$"-wide regular (nondecorative, or "lipped") or clear elastic will do the trick. There are two ways to deal with regular elastic. You can fold back a hem and fill the tube you created with the elastic, so the elastic is essentially loose inside the tube. The other way is to treat the elastic the same way as tape: Stick the elastic through the slot on the foot and serge it to the fabric's edge so the elastic is encased in the overlock stitches. You can stretch the elastic as you sew so it gathers up the fabric (this is great for puff sleeves, the waists of full skirts, and the bottoms of bubble skirts), or you can sew it flat, for things like waists of skirts that you want to lie flat.

Some elastics have a lip with a decorative scalloped edge. This lip is the seam allowance for the decorative edge. Those can just be serged on. Check out some of your tank tops or underwear, and you'll probably see what I'm talking about.

Encased elastic

1. Using an overlock stitch (or zigzag), sew elastic to the wrong side of the fabric. Do this by inserting elastic into the slot of the presser foot or just laying it under the presser foot. The overlock stitches will envelop the elastic.

2. Fold back the edge so the elastic is encased in the hem.

3. Topstitch with either a zigzag or a straight stitch, stretching the elastic out as you topstitch so the topstitch won't break when the elastic stretches on your body. Hint: Use a cover-stitch machine here, if possible, for best results.

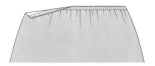

Elastic with lip

1. Using an overlock stitch, sew the lip of the elastic to the face of the garment.

2. Turn the elastic back so the decorative edge is the new edge of the garment, giving a clean, finished look.

3. Topstitch below the decorative edge on the garment body to secure the overlocked lip to the body.

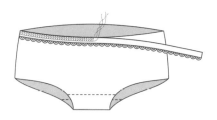

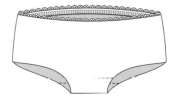

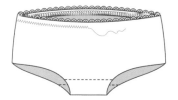

▱▱▱▱▱▱	**RIGHT SIDE ELASTIC**
▱▱▱▱▱▱	**WRONG SIDE ELASTIC**

BINDING

Another way to finish a raw edge is by binding. This is similar to the way we bind woven fabrics. Usually we use binding for necklines, and sometimes we use it for hems or armholes. It's also good to use binding for a contrast look, or if you can't find matching ribbing to finish the edge.

There a few different ways to bind. First is the **full bind**, in which the binding has clean, folded-in edges with the garment's raw edge inserted inside. Then there is the **mock bind**, where the outside has a clean, folded edge and the inside is the raw edge covered with an overlock stitch. There are variations of both styles, depending on the topstitching style and placement. One other variable is the finished rib width, which depends on how wide you cut your rib in the first place but also on how much you fold it back; just over the seam allowance will give you a ¼" finished rib width, for example.

Full bind

1. Cut a 1" strip of fabric. If you have a small area that needs stretch, use a rib fabric for the binding.

2. With right sides together, stitch the binding to the neckline, using either overlock or zigzag stitches.

3. Fold back the binding's raw edge, then fold over once more to cover the neck seam.

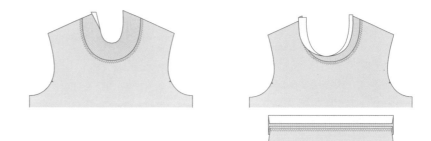

4. Topstitch the binding. Here I chose a zigzag on the binding, but you can use a cover stitch if you have that machine.

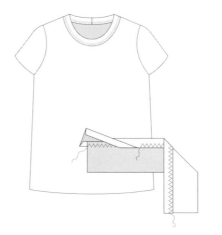
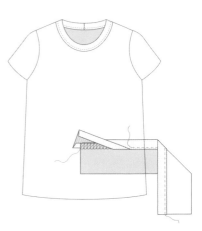

Mock bind

1. Cut a 1″ strip of fabric. If you have a small area that needs stretch, use a rib fabric for the binding. Finish one raw edge of binding using an overlock stitch (or mock overlock if you don't have a serger).

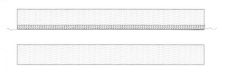

2. With right sides together, stitch the binding to the neckline using either overlock or zigzag stitches.

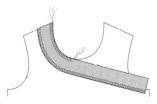

3. Fold back the binding so it's at the desired height.

4. Topstitch the binding using the desired topstitch and placement. Here I chose a zigzag stitch below the binding for a narrow neckline.

Binding width

Try cutting your binding wider or narrower.

Try folding it back below the seam line, or just matching it up so that it's "kissing" the seam line, as shown here.

STITCHING STYLE AND POSITION

You can use a zigzag or straight stitch for topstitching the binding. If the area needs stretch, I recommend using a zigzag, or else your straight stitches will rip right out. The best choice is a cover stitch, if you have one.

You can topstitch on top of the binding or on the body of the garment just below the binding—it all depends on the look you want to achieve. If you decide to topstitch on the body, make sure the binding dips below the seam so that you can catch it while you topstitch. Most full bindings topstitch on top of the binding, since it is usually lined up against the seam and doesn't dip below. You can let it dip slightly below and run a topstitch—usually a straight stitch—in the seam line between the binding and the garment body. This is called "stitch in the ditch" and secures the binding but leaves a hidden stitch line.

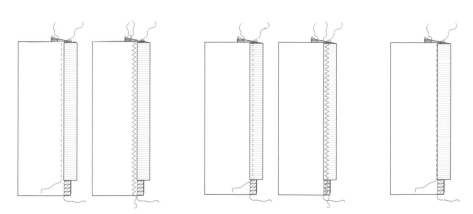

RIBBING

This is the technique utilized in traditional T-shirts, and it's a really easy way to finish edges of all sorts. Since a strip of ribbing is folded in half, the folded part creates a clean finish. This strip is serged to the raw edge of a neckline, sleeve, or hem, so you don't need a cover-stitch machine. You can just use a serger or at the very least a zigzag stitch, which won't show. In fact, when you use ribbing to finish edges, there isn't really any topstitching showing anywhere. This application is similar to the way you apply decorative elastic with a lip.

There are two ways to sew on ribbing. One is super-easy, and you will have an inside seam showing. The other is a clean, finished rib where no seams are showing.

The super-easy rib

1. Sew the front and back shoulders of your garment together on one side. (Do not sew both shoulders, since you'll need an opening at the neck to sew on the ribbing.)

2. Fold the strip in half lengthwise. If your strip is 2″ wide, fold it so that it's 1″ wide.

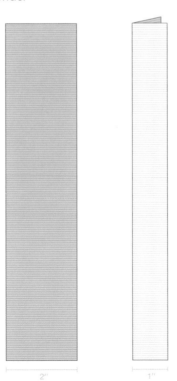

3. Place the raw edges of the folded rib on the face of the garment neck. Serge it around the neckline, going over the shoulder seam and around to the end of the neck.

4. Sew the other shoulder together from armhole to neck rib, thus stitching together the neck rib and finishing the neckline.

The clean rib

1. Sew both shoulders of the garment together.

2. Sew the rib ends together, forming a long loop.

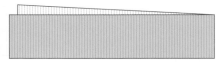

RIGHT SIDE OF RIB

WRONG SIDE OF RIB

3. Fold the rib loop in half lengthwise (making it 1″ wide if it's 2″ wide), wrong side to wrong side, so the seam you made is encased.

4. Divide the loop into 4 equal

sections. The seam line of the rib will be the center back. Mark the points for the center front and shoulders.

5. Pin this rib circle at the pointed marks to the points on your shirt neckline's face.

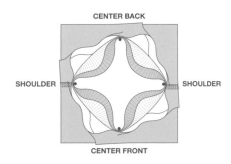

CENTER BACK

SHOULDER — SHOULDER

CENTER FRONT

6. Sew around the entire neckline, stretching the rib to fit into the neckline as you go.

TIP

Rib trim should never be as long as the raw edge it's being sewn to—you will stretch it out as you sew. Generally speaking, 1-by-1 ribs should measure about two thirds the length of the space they should fit into. So if your neckline is 18″, the rib should be 12″ when flat and then be stretched into the 18″ space. You will serge the ribbed trim to the raw garment edge, right side to right side. Important: Pull the ribbed trim as you serge so that it stretches out.

If you've never used this technique before, practice using spare fabric before you attempt it on a garment you've already sewn together.

FACING AND LINING

As with woven garments, you can create a clean, finished edge by attaching a facing or lining—a mirror-image layer of fabric that falls on the inside of the garment. This might not be a technique you use with T-shirts and layering tanks, since you might not want more than one layer of fabric, but for something like a cold-weather-appropriate tank dress or a square-necked wool jersey dress it makes sense. You can make these out of the garment fabric, or use a silky, skin-friendly stretchy nylon or polyester tricot, like you find in lingerie. You can line your garment with anything, as long as it's stretchy and lightweight. Lining isn't very common when sewing knits, but it's an option. You might notice that your swimsuit is lined with a skin-colored tricot fabric. Sometimes it's good to line a pale knit dress so that it's not see-through.

Simply serge or zigzag stitch (with a conventional machine) the facing or lining to the garment. Make sure the right sides are together. Turn the facing or lining inside the garment and press the seam inside out. You can also secure the facing or lining inside the garment by understitching it and then tacking the corners to the inside shoulder seams with a quick hand stitch.

Pressing

A nice thing about sewing knits is that because of their stretchy nature, you don't really need to press open each and every seam with an iron after you sew it, as you do with wovens. Because knits are much more flexible than wovens, you can pull the seams flat while sewing, whereas wovens usually need a little more muscle to flatten them. If you're creating a topstitched hem, you'll want to press it once you've folded it back, before topstitching. Sometimes, if it's a narrow hem, you can just eyeball it and fold it back with your fingers as you sew. After sewing, just do a final press.

Buttonholes, Zippers, and Closures

Whether you're working with knits or wovens, you need to stabilize the immediate vicinity before you make a buttonhole, sew a zipper, or attach a button. Since knit fabric is much drapier and flimsier than woven fabric, it's important to firm up the areas that are carrying a load. I recommend using knitted tricot fusible interfacing. Check your local fabric store for lightweight fusible interfacings that work well with knits. If your fabric has synthetic stretch fibers woven in, be sure to opt for a low-heat fusible interfacing so you don't melt your brand-new poly-blend top!

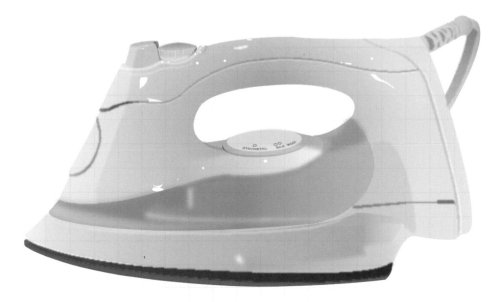

CHAPTER 6
TEEING OFF

An Eight-Step Program for the World's Easiest T-shirt

NOW THAT YOU KNOW ALL ABOUT HOW TO SEW STRETCH FABRICS, ARE YOU READY TO CRANK OUT THE SIMPLEST T-SHIRT EVER?

This is my time-tested formula, and one I hope you'll refer to again and again over the years. I'll break it down for beginners, experienced sewers, and experts. On your mark, get set, go!

- Buy cotton jersey fabric. Depending on the fabric's width, buy 1 yard (for 45″ fabric) or 3/4 yard (for 60″ fabric). Medium and advanced sewers, buy a quarter of a yard of 1/4″-wide cotton tape for stabilizing and half a yard of ribbing for neck and/or sleeves.

- Wash and dry the fabric to preshrink.

- Lay the jersey out on your table, flat and open.

- Let it sit for an hour or so to recover its natural state. Washing, stretching, and folding tend to leave knit fabric all bent out of shape.

PREPPING FABRIC

CUTTING

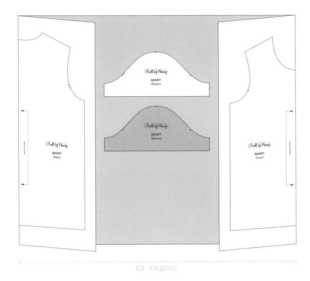

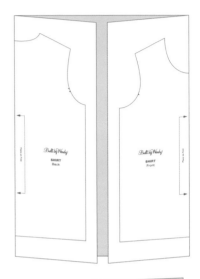

- Fold each lengthwise edge in the width of the pattern piece.

- Lay one sleeve faceup and the other reversed.

- Cut rib pieces if you are doing the medium or advanced version. (Fold the rib in half, right side out; lay pattern pieces on the fold and cut.)

NOTE

Rib needed for medium and advanced projects.

- Fold the fabric in thirds (right side out). Lay front and back patterns on each fold and secure them with weights or pins. Cut the pieces out.

- Take the remaining fabric, unfold the thirds, and refold it in half.

- Lay the sleeve pattern pieces and cut out.

SETTING UP
SET UP YOUR MACHINE TO SEW

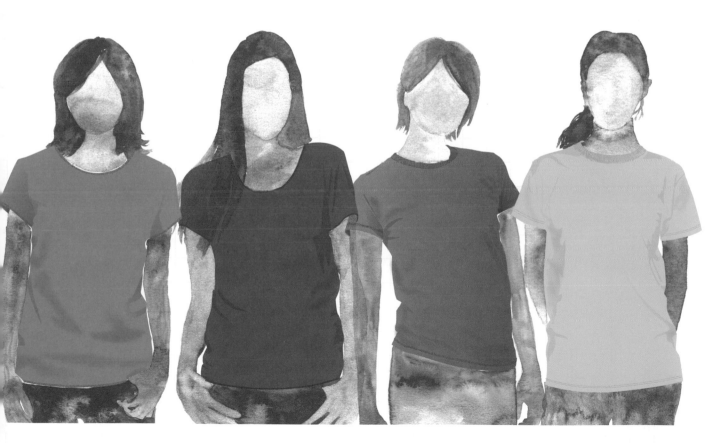

Tee with Overlocked Edges

Easiest: Set up your serger for a 3-thread overlock stitch, narrow width, using three cones of matching thread (or two matching cones and one fabric-matching spool with spool lid). If you don't have a serger, set up your conventional machine for a narrow zigzag stitch, using a spool of matching thread. Substitute the zigzag (or mock overlock, if you have it) stitch wherever it says "overlock" in the following instructions.

TIP

Try using contrast thread.

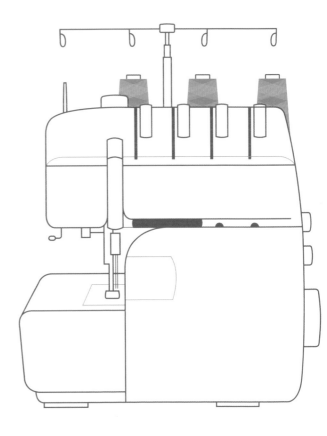

SEWING STEPS: EASIEST

1	2	3	4
With right sides together, overlock (or zig-zag) the front and back pieces together at the left shoulder.	Overlock (or zigzag) around the neck hole.	With right sides together, overlock (or zigzag) the front and back pieces together at the right shoulder.	With right sides together, overlock (or zigzag) the sleeves to the armholes.

5	6	7	8
Overlock (or zigzag) the sleeve opening.	With right sides together, overlock (or zig-zag) front and back pieces together at left side from the bottom hem up to the sleeve opening.	Overlock around the bottom opening.	With right sides together, overlock (or zigzag) front and back pieces together at left side from the bottom up to the sleeve opening.

Tee with Roll Hem Edges

Easy: Set up your serger for a 3-thread overlock stitch, narrow width, using three cones of matching thread (or two matching cones and one fabric-matching spool with spool lid) and one spool of decorative thread to switch out later for your rolled hems.

TIP

Try using decorative thread.

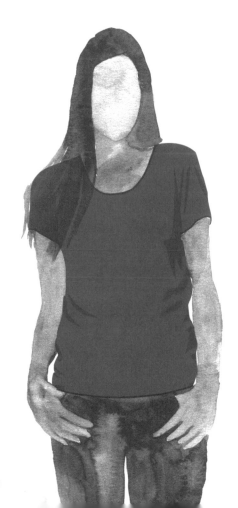

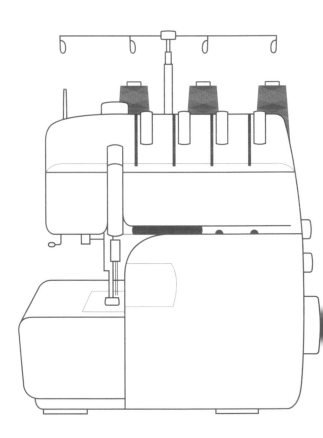

SEWING STEPS: EASY

1	2	3	4
With right sides together, overlock the front and back pieces together at the left shoulder.	Roll-hem stitch around the neck hole, using decorative thread.	With right sides together, overlock the front and back pieces together at the right shoulder.	With right sides together, overlock the sleeves to the armholes.

5	6	7	8
Roll-hem stitch the sleeve openings, using decorative thread.	With right sides together, overlock front and back pieces together at the left side from the bottom opening up to the sleeve opening.	Roll-hem stitch the bottom opening, using decorative thread.	With right sides together, overlock front and back pieces together at right side from the bottom up to the sleeve openings.

Tee with Ribbed Neck

Medium: Set up your serger for a 3-thread overlock stitch, narrow width, using three cones of matching thread (or two matching cones and one fabric-matching spool with spool lid). Set up your conventional machine with fabric-matching spool and bobbin thread.

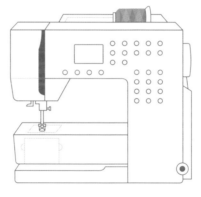

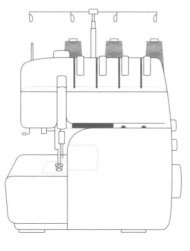

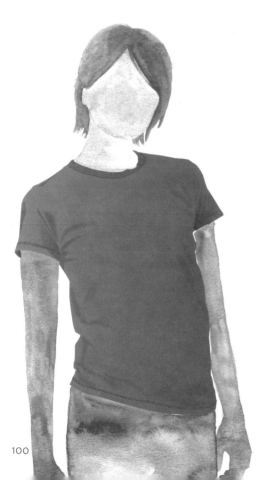

SEWING STEPS: MEDIUM

1	2	3	4
With right sides together, overlock the front and back pieces together at the left shoulder, inserting tape into the seam.	Fold rib in half lengthwise (wrong sides together) and overlock the raw edges of the rib to the right side of neck hole.	With right sides together, overlock the front and back pieces together at the right shoulder (and neck rib), inserting tape into the seam.	With right sides together, overlock the sleeves to the armholes.

5	6	7	8
Overlock the sleeve openings, fold them back, and topstitch their hems (using the conventional machine) with zigzag stitch.	With right sides together, overlock front and back pieces together at the left side from the bottom opening up to the sleeve hem.	Overlock the bottom opening, fold back, and topstitch the hem (using a conventional machine) using a zigzag stitch.	With right sides together, overlock front and back pieces together at the right side from the bottom hem up to the sleeve hem.

Tee with Coverstitched Hem

Advanced: Set up your serger for a
3-thread overlock stitch, narrow width,
using three cones of matching thread
(or two matching cones and one fabric-
matching spool with spool lid). Set up
your cover-stitch machine with fabric-
matching cones of thread.

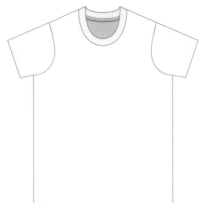

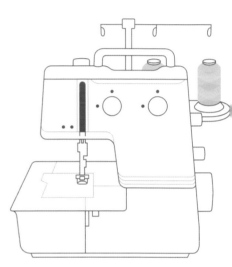

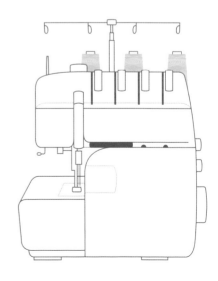

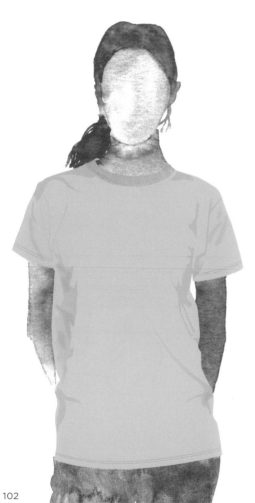

SEWING STEPS: ADVANCED

1	2	3	4
With right sides together, overlock the front and back pieces together at both shoulders, inserting tape into the seams.	Fold the rib in half (right sides together), overlock the seam, and fold in half lengthwise with the wrong sides together, hiding the seam.	Overlock the neck rib's raw edges to the right side of the neck opening, pinning it at center front, center back, and shoulder points for even spreading. Stretch the neck rib as you sew.	With right sides together, overlock the sleeves to the armholes.

5	6	7	8
Fold back the sleeve openings and cover-stitch their hems.	With right sides together, overlock front and back pieces together at the left side from the bottom opening up to the sleeve hem.	Fold back the bottom opening and cover-stitch the hem.	With right sides together, overlock front and back pieces together at the right side from the bottom hem up to the sleeve hem.

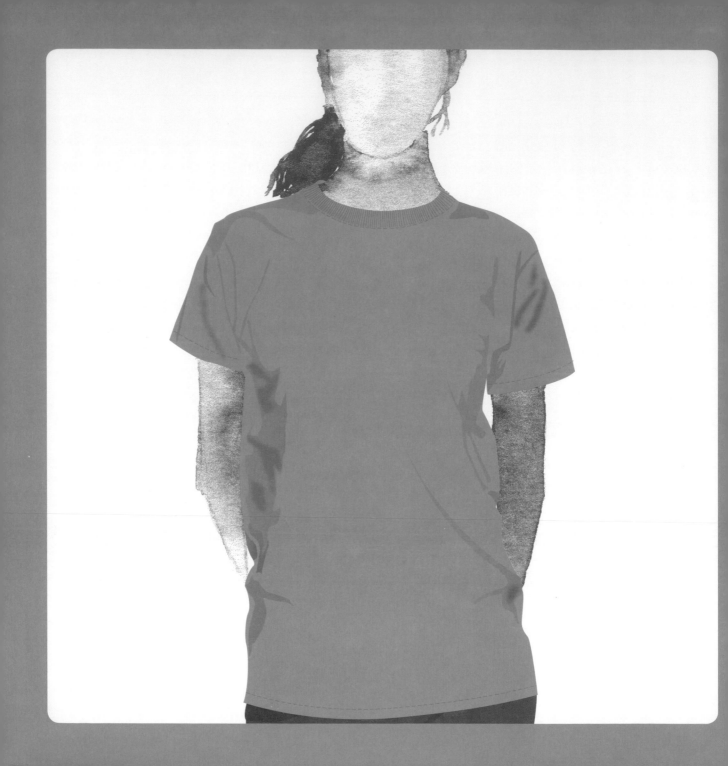

CHAPTER 7
THE CREWNECK

Beyond the Basic Tee

NOW THAT YOU'VE CREATED YOUR FIRST T-SHIRT, YOU WON'T BELIEVE HOW MANY DIRECTIONS YOU CAN TAKE IT IN.

This chapter will give you the knowledge and ideas to use what you've just learned and kick it up a notch. What if you could make dressier, more feminine pieces with the same effortless, slip-on-and-be-done, so-cozy-you-can-sleep-in-it quality as your favorite T-shirt? The great news is, you can—and it's easier than you might think.

The crewneck tee is the most basic of knitwear patterns, and that's why it's the perfect place for us to start customizing patterns and details. For such a simple garment, it has so many variables that can be customized: You can change the shape of the neckline, remove the sleeves, add length to make a tunic or even a dress, and play around with fabrics and trims. With the slightest of changes, you can create dozens of different looks—and some of them are so interesting that you won't even believe that the basic T-shirt pattern was the source! The only limit is your own imagination.

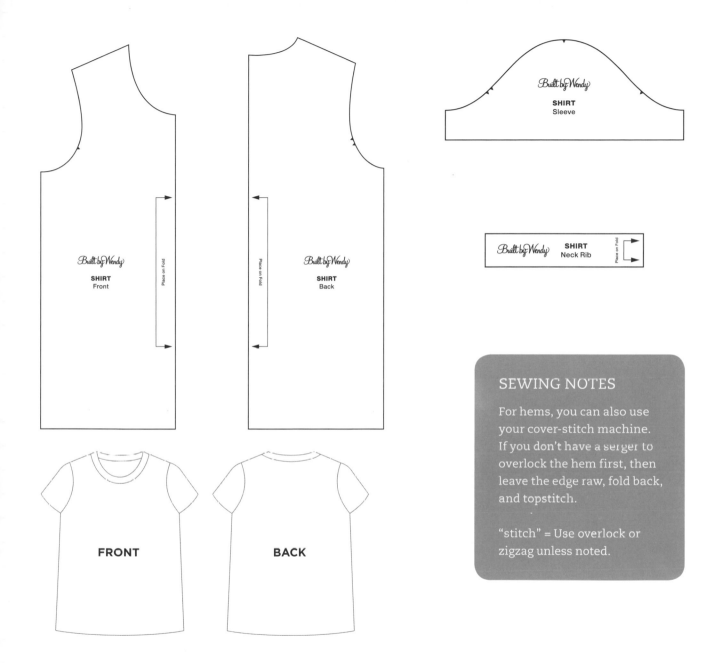

Built by Wendy

SHIRT
Sleeve

Built by Wendy

SHIRT
Front

Place on Fold

Built by Wendy

SHIRT
Back

Place on Fold

Built by Wendy **SHIRT** Neck Rib

Place on Fold

FRONT

BACK

SEWING NOTES

For hems, you can also use your cover-stitch machine. If you don't have a serger to overlock the hem first, then leave the edge raw, fold back, and topstitch.

"stitch" = Use overlock or zigzag unless noted.

PATTERN PIECES

BUILT BY YOU
PROJECTS

These projects may take the basic
T-shirt pattern beyond what you
ever thought possible, but that
doesn't mean you should think of
them as the be-all and end-all of
tee tweaking. Feel free to mix and
match the various techniques and
detail suggestions for each project
to design your own totally original
creations. Add buttons, trim, appliqués, or any other bells and whistles
you can dream up!

Project #1:
Tank Girl

If I had the space in my modest
Manhattan closet, I'd want to own
hundreds of tank tops. This simple
layer is incredibly versatile and
flattering. Worn with jeans, skirts,
and shorts, it's the backbone of
any summer wardrobe, but it works
just as well layered under cozy fall
cardigans, paired with pajama pants
for sleeping, or partnered with yoga
pants for exercising. This version is
just the kind I want to wear: slender,
with straps that are just the right
width and a scoop neckline that's
neither too high nor too low.

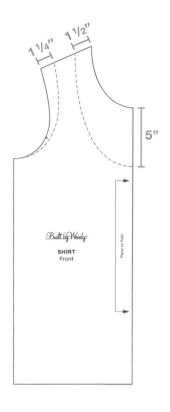

1¼" 1½"

5"

1½" 1¼"

6"

Supplies

1 yard jersey
¼ yard rib

Pattern Adjustments

1. Drop the neckline at center front 5″ and at shoulder 1½″. Draw a new neckline.

2. Move the shoulder (for front and back pieces) in 1¼″. Redraw the armhole.

3. Drop the back neckline at center back 6″ and at the shoulder 1½″. Draw a new neckline.

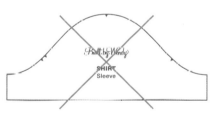

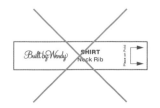

CUTTING

Cut out the pattern pieces shown.
Also, cut three 2″ by 15″ strips for
neckline and armhole binding.

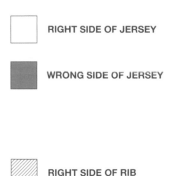

RIGHT SIDE OF JERSEY

WRONG SIDE OF JERSEY

RIGHT SIDE OF RIB

WRONG SIDE OF RIB

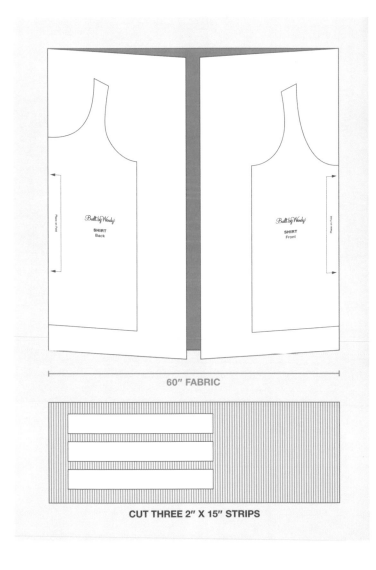

60″ FABRIC

CUT THREE 2″ X 15″ STRIPS

SEWING

1. With right sides together, stitch the front body to the back body at the left shoulder seam.

2. Fold the neck ribbing in half lengthwise and stitch the raw edge of the ribbing to the right side of the neckhole.

3. With right sides together, stitch the front and back body pieces at the right shoulder seam, including neck ribbing.

4. Stitch ribbing around the armholes the same way you did with the neck hole.

5. With right sides together, stitch the front body to the back body at the side seams, including armhole ribbing.

6. Overlock the raw edge of the hem, fold back 1", and topstitch with a zigzag stitch.

1

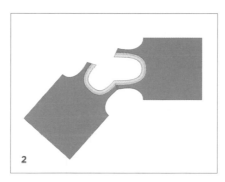

2

3

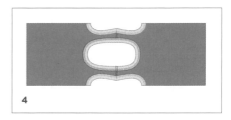

4

5

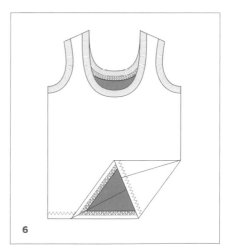

6

Project #2:
Get the Scoop

The T-shirt may be a unisex invention, but this updated version is anything but. With its feminine, curve-enhancing drape, it can be dressed up or down, day or night. It looks sexy and modern, but it's incredibly comfortable. It's also layerable: try a tank beneath it for contrast or a hint of extra warmth. My version has an elastic hem for a blouson effect, but as always, feel free to play around with the details.

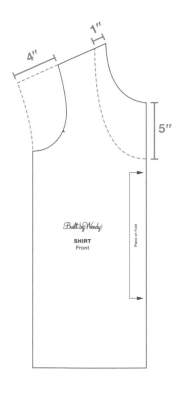

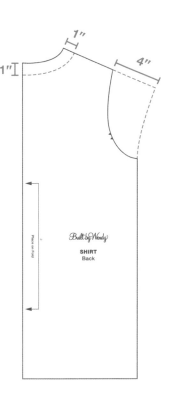

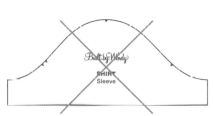

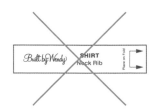

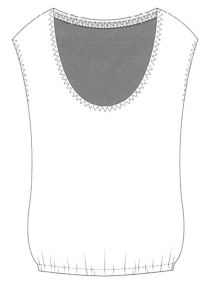

Supplies

1 yard jersey (horizontal stripes are nice with this style)

2 yards ¼" standard or clear elastic

1 yard ½" elastic

Pattern Adjustments

1. Drop the front neckline 5" at the center point and 1" at the shoulder. Draw a new neckline.

2. Drop the back neckline 1" all around. Draw a new back neckline.

3. Extend the shoulder seams 4" on both front and back and square off to meet the bottom armhole.

CUTTING

Cut out the pattern pieces shown.

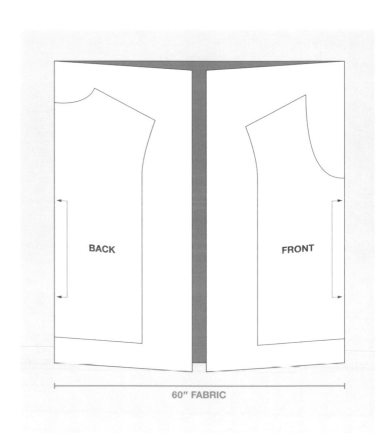

BACK

FRONT

60" FABRIC

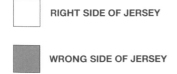

RIGHT SIDE OF JERSEY

WRONG SIDE OF JERSEY

SEWING

1. With right sides together, stitch the front body to the back body at the left shoulder. For this style, you might want to add tape in the shoulder seam for more support.

2. Stitch ¼" elastic to the wrong side of the neck opening's raw edge. Pin it in place first if you're scared.

3. With right sides together, stitch the front body to the back body at the right shoulder.

4. Turn back the neck opening, folding the elastic inside the hem, and topstitch (zigzag or straight stitch).

5. Overlock the armholes, fold back ½", and topstitch (zigzag).

6. With right sides together, stitch the front and back body pieces together at the left side seam.

7. Overlock the bottom hem, fold back 1", topstitch (straight stitch or zigzag), and fill with ½" elastic. To determine the amount of waist elastic to use, take your yard of ½" elastic and wrap it around the lower part of your waist. Cut the length that is comfortable. Attach a safety pin to the end of the elastic, slip it into the tube, and work it through—just like rethreading a drawstring in your sweatpants.

8. With right sides together, stitch the front and back pieces together at the right side seam.

1

2

3

4

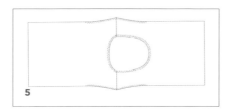

5

6

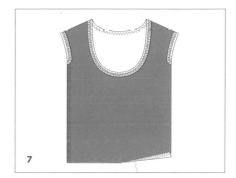

7

8

Project #3:
V All That You Can V

This deep V shape is very flattering for most body types. The cap sleeves are a cute counterbalance to the dramatic neckline, and the little piece of elastic in the center front makes the V a bit more interesting. This style is great in solid colors, but you might also try prints or sheers.

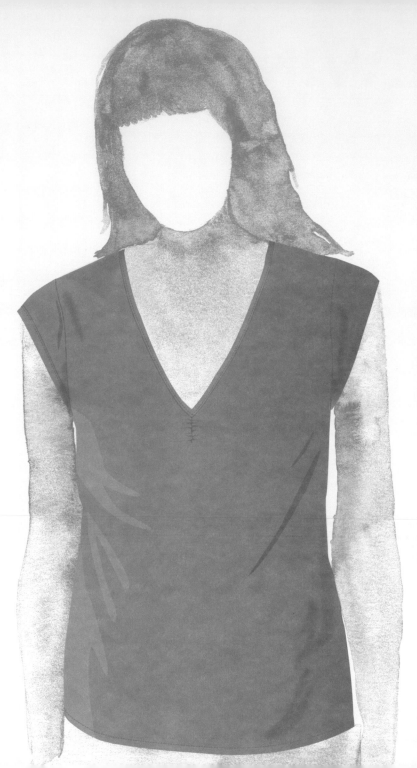

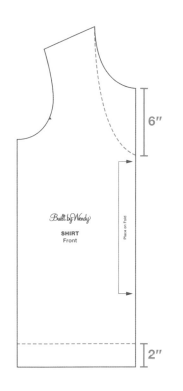

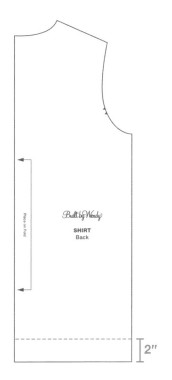

6″

2″

2″

Built by Wendy

SHIRT
Front

Place on Fold

Place on Fold

Built by Wendy

SHIRT
Back

Supplies

1 yard jersey
3″ of ⅛″ elastic

Pattern Adjustments

1. Drop the front neckline 6″ at the center point. Redraw the neckline.

2. Raise the sleeve hem 2″ at the center and 1″ at the sides. Redraw the hem.

3. Shorten the hem of the front and back pattern pieces 2″, as shown.

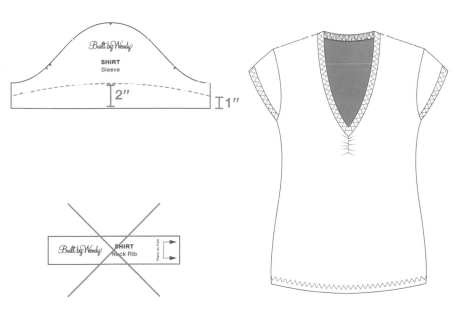

Built by Wendy

SHIRT
Sleeve

2″

1″

Built by Wendy

SHIRT
Neck Rib

Place on Fold

CUTTING

Cut out the pattern pieces shown and three 1" by 17" strips for binding. Cut these strips on the fold to make things easier. This binding length will cover a range of sizes, so if you're making a smaller garment, you might have to trim off some of the extra binding.

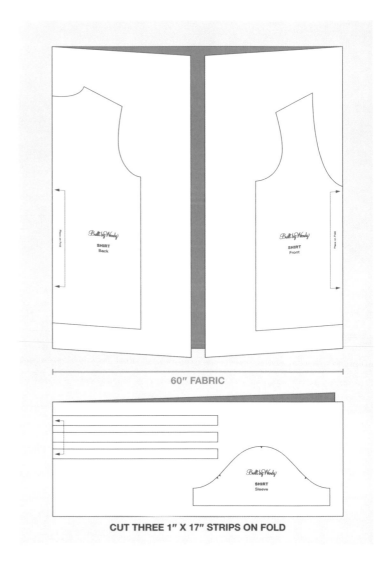

60" FABRIC

CUT THREE 1" X 17" STRIPS ON FOLD

RIGHT SIDE OF JERSEY

WRONG SIDE OF JERSEY

SEWING

1. With right sides together, stitch the front body to the back body at the left shoulder.

2. On the wrong side of the front piece, straight-stitch the 3″ strip of elastic in the center just below the neckline, pulling as you sew to gather it up.

3. Stitch binding around the neck opening. I use a mock bind here, but feel free to try another binding version if you prefer (see chapter 5).

4. With right sides together, stitch the front and back pieces together at the right shoulder.

5. With right sides together, stitch the sleeves to the armholes.

6. Stitch binding around the sleeve openings. Use mock bind or whichever version you prefer.

7. With right sides together, stitch front and back pieces together at the side seams.

8. Overlock the bottom hem, fold back 1″, and topstitch (zigzag or cover stitch).

1

2

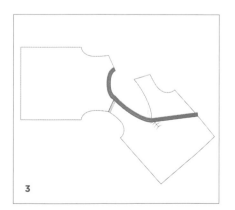

3

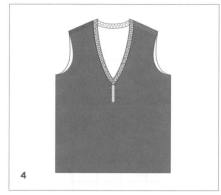

4

5

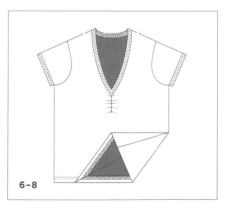

6-8

Project #4:
Rock the Boatneck

Who doesn't love a boatneck? This classic nautical style is preppy, polished, and universally flattering. You can make it in colorful stripes or solids, or even add a cute iron-on appliqué on the chest to make it look like a vintage find you unearthed somewhere along the coast of Maine.

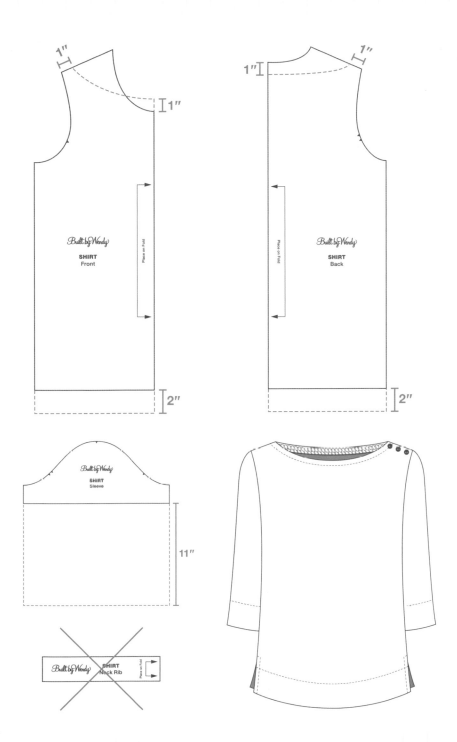

Supplies

1 ½ yards striped jersey

3 small gold buttons (18–24 line size)

Pattern Adjustments

1. Raise the front neckline 1″ at the center.

2. Drop the back neckline 1″ at the center.

3. Measure 1″ in from the shoulder on front and back pieces.

4. Draw a wide neckline from the new shoulder points to the center neck points.

5. Add 11″ to the sleeve length. Square off the new sleeve length.

6. Add 2″ to the front and back length.

CUTTING

Cut out the pattern pieces shown
and cut a 1″ by 10″ strip (on the fold)
for the neck binding.

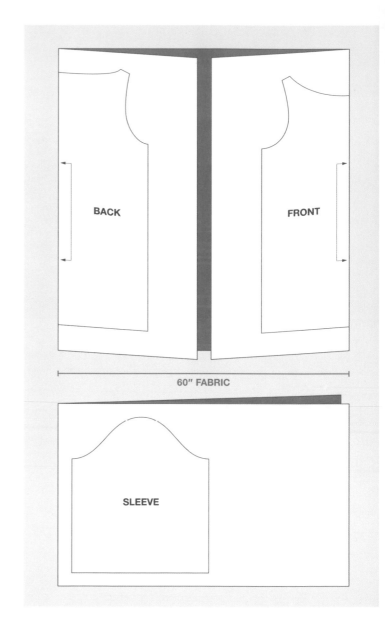

BACK

FRONT

60″ FABRIC

SLEEVE

RIGHT SIDE OF JERSEY

WRONG SIDE OF JERSEY

SEWING

1. With right sides together, stitch the front body to the back body at the left shoulder.

2. Overlock neck raw edge, fold back, and topstitch.

3. With right sides together, stitch the front and back body pieces together at the right shoulder.

4. With right sides together, stitch the sleeves to the armholes.

5. Overlock the sleeve opening.

6. With right sides together, stitch the front and back pieces together at the side seams, from the notch where the slit begins to the sleeve opening.

7. Overlock the bottom and slit opening raw edges.

8. Fold back the side slits and the bottom and sleeve openings 2″. Topstitch with a straight stitch going around the slit opening.

9. Attach buttons along the right shoulder seam to create a decorative mock buttoned shoulder.

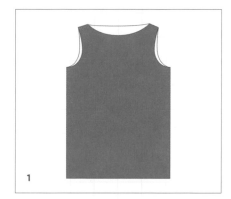

1

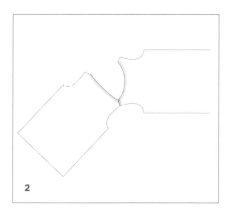

2

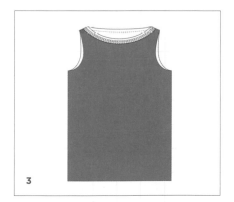

3

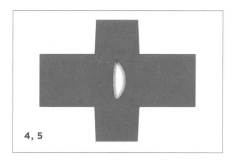

4, 5

6

7

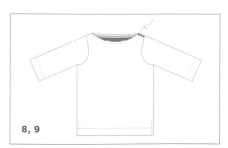

8, 9

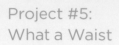

Project #5:
What a Waist

Sometimes you want the ease of a
T-shirt but a look that's a little bit more
polished. This updated shape, which
has the feeling of a woven blouse, is
the perfect option for dressing up
your jeans. Try belting it or layering it
beneath a tailored vest.

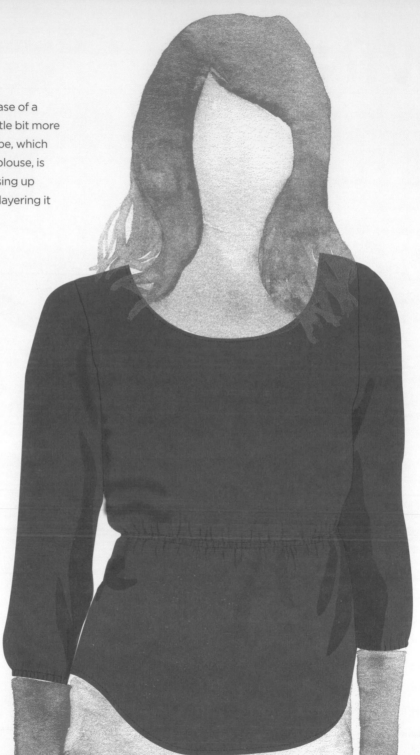

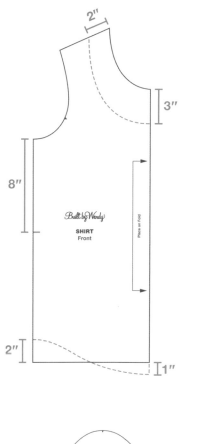

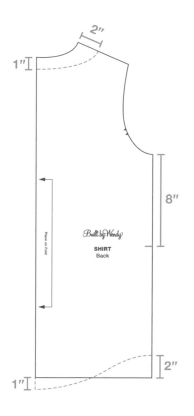

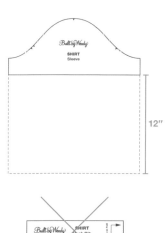

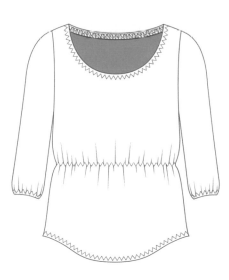

Supplies

1 ½ yards jersey
2 yards ¼" elastic

Pattern Adjustments

1. Drop the neckline 3" at the center front and 2" at the shoulder. Draw a new neckline.

2. Drop the neckline 1" at the center back and 2" at the shoulder. Draw a new neckline.

3. Drop the front and back hems 1" at the center and shorten them at the side seams by 2". Draw a new shaped hem.

4. Mark a notch on the front and back side seams, 8" down from the armhole. This indicates where the elastic for the waist will go.

5. Add 12" to the sleeve length.

CUTTING

Cut out the pattern pieces shown.

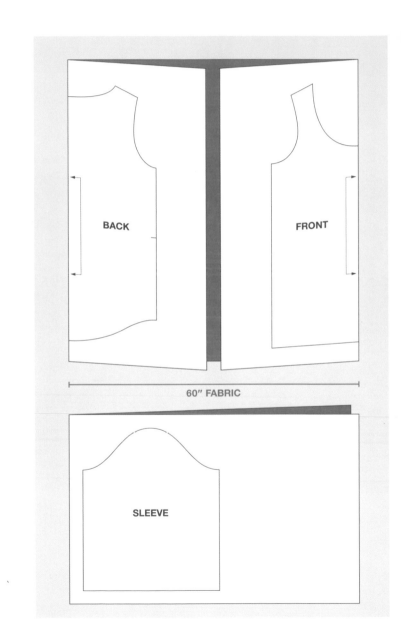

60" FABRIC

BACK

FRONT

SLEEVE

RIGHT SIDE OF JERSEY

WRONG SIDE OF JERSEY

SEWING

1. With right sides together, stitch the front body to the back body at the left shoulder.

2. Stitch elastic to the wrong side of the neck opening's raw edge.

3. With right sides together, stitch the front and back pieces together at the right shoulder.

4. Fold back the neck opening and topstitch (zigzag, straight stitch, or cover stitch).

5. With right sides together, stitch the sleeves to the armholes.

6. Stitch elastic to the wrong side of the sleeve opening's raw edge, stretching the elastic as you sew. Use anywhere from 9″ to 10 ½″ per sleeve, depending how tight you want them.

7. Topstitch (zigzag) elastic between the waist notches on the wrong sides of the front and back pieces. Use anywhere between 13″ and 16″ of elastic on each piece. Pull the elastic as you sew.

8. Overlock the bottom hem, fold back 1″, and topstitch (zigzag or cover-stitch).

9. With right sides together, stitch front and back pieces together at the side seams from the bottom up to the sleeve openings.

10. Fold back the sleeve openings ¼″, enclosing elastic in the hem. Topstitch (zigzag) while stretching the hem.

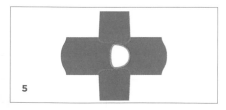

Project #6:
Mini Me

Minidresses are my secret wardrobe weapon. There's no better way to throw something on, run out of the house, and still look adorable. This design makes for a great daytime spring dress in plain cotton jersey or interlock, and it works just as well as a beach cover-up when made with terry cloth. Or try something completely different and make one in a slinky metallic rayon jersey for a chic cocktail-party look. This pattern also enables you to try out some more advanced sewing techniques. Why not test your skills and create a design that allows you to make facing and pocket pieces? And remember, anytime you have a facing, you can use that seam to insert pipings or ruffles, so don't be afraid to experiment!

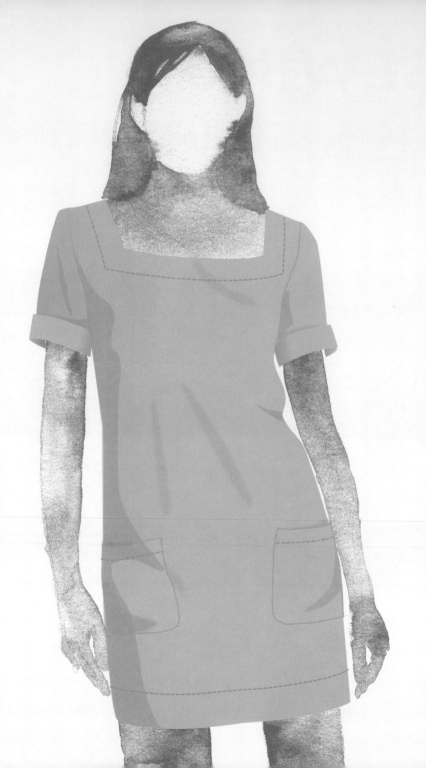

Supplies

2 ½ yards printed jersey

1 yard white tricot fusible interfacing

Pattern Adjustments

Front

1. Lower the neckline 1 ¼" at the center front and 1 ¼" at the shoulders. Square off the new points (or try a different shape if you want).

2. Mark the facing shape line 1 ½" away from the new neckline.

3. Mark a point 1 ½" out from the side seam at the hem. Trace a diagonal line from 9 ½" above the hem at the side to this point, and continue the line until it reaches 6" below the hem line.

4. Drop the center front hem 6".

5. Draw a shaped line to connect these points and form the new hem.

6. Mark the pocket shape 1" from the side seam and 8" above the hem.

Back

Follow steps 1–5 for the back.

Facings and Pocket

Trace the shape of the facings and transfer them to form new pattern pieces.

Sleeve

Add 6" to sleeve length and square off the new hem. Make a notch 3" up from the new hem to mark where you will fold it back.

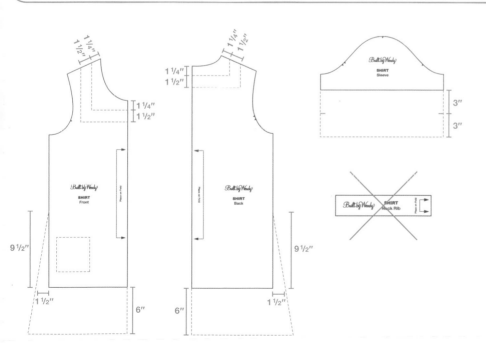

CUTTING

Cut out the pattern pieces shown
plus the new pieces (the facings and
the pockets).

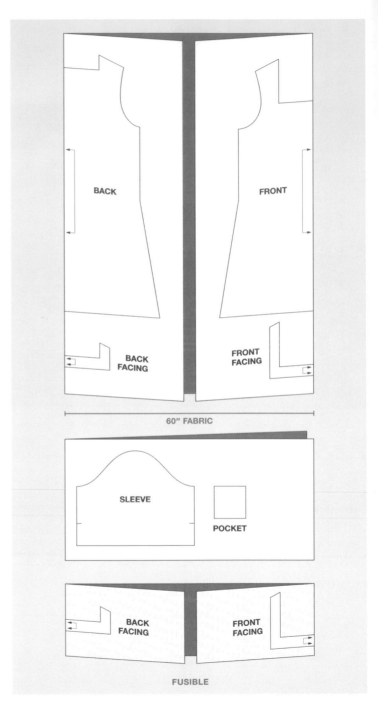

BACK

FRONT

BACK
FACING

FRONT
FACING

60" FABRIC

SLEEVE

POCKET

BACK
FACING

FRONT
FACING

FUSIBLE

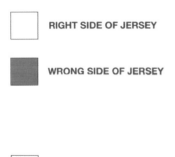

RIGHT SIDE OF JERSEY

WRONG SIDE OF JERSEY

RIGHT SIDE OF FUSIBLE

WRONG SIDE OF FUSIBLE

SEWING

1. Fuse the interfacing to the wrong side of the facings.

2. With right sides together, stitch the front and back body pieces together at the shoulder. Do the same with the facings. Overlock the raw outer edges of the facings.

3. With right sides together, stitch the facing neck opening to the body neck opening. Turn the facing inside the body. Topstitch (straight-stitch) the facing to the body.

4. With right sides together, stitch the sleeves to the armholes. Overlock the sleeve openings' raw edges.

5. Fold and topstitch (straight-stitch) the pockets' top raw edges. Fold the pocket seam allowances inward and press. Topstitch (straight-stitch) the pockets to the front body.

6. With right sides together, stitch the front and back pieces together at the side seams from the bottom opening to the sleeve opening.

7. Overlock the bottom opening, fold back 3″, and topstitch (straight-stitch or cover-stitch).

8. Fold back each sleeve opening 3″ to create a wide hem and topstitch (zigzag or cover-stitch). Roll up each sleeve 2″ to make a cuff.

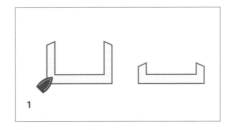

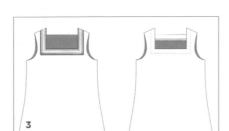

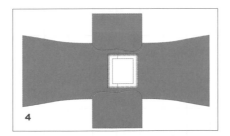

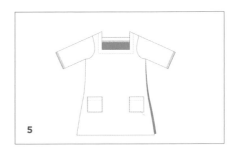

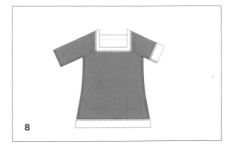

CHAPTER 8
THE RAGLAN

Designing with a Bold Shoulder

YOU MAY KNOW THAT A RAGLAN TOP HAS SLEEVES WITH SEAMS THAT ANGLE INWARD FOR A DISTINCTIVE, SPORTY LOOK.

You may not know that this type of pattern can be altered to make loads of interesting garments besides the basic sweatshirt.

Sure, we all love our baseball tees and heather-gray fleece pullovers, but who knew you could make a halter top or a peasant dress from the very same pattern? With a few simple tweaks, this classic shape can be used to create plenty of not-so-classic high-fashion pieces. This chapter will explore a variety of options, from a chic beach cover-up to a *Flashdance*-style shoulder-exposing fleece top. And, of course, I include one of the most useful garments known to man: the hoodie. Because of the way the sleeve seams work, you can find new ways to experiment with trims, adding ruffles or color-ful pipings. Or try playing with proportion—make sleeves longer or shorter, or make a full-length dress or a half-shirt. With some minor pattern-making, you can widen your pattern to make a full, gathered loose blouse from the same basic pattern as your slim-fit T-shirt. You can also use color blocking for a sporty look. We'll cover a range of looks in this chapter, but my suggestions are only suggestions.

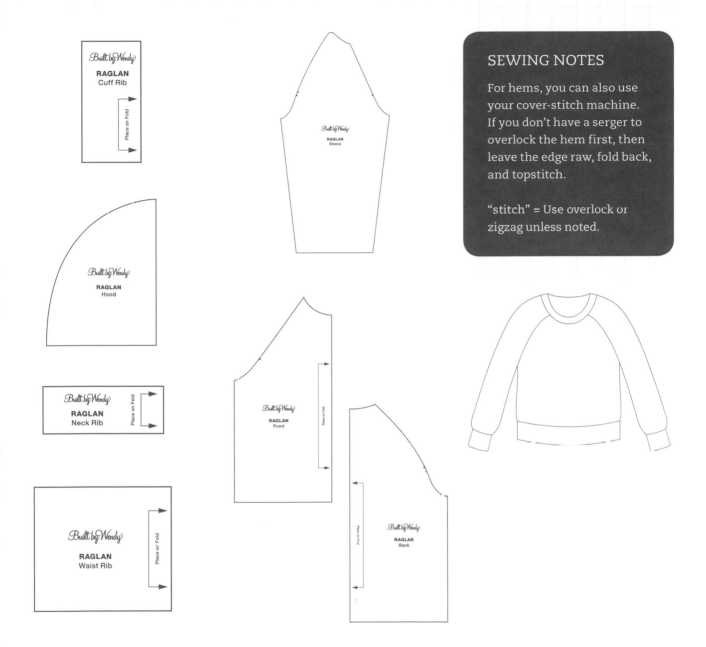

Built by Wendy
RAGLAN
Cuff Rib

Place on Fold

Built by Wendy
RAGLAN
Sleeve

Built by Wendy
RAGLAN
Hood

Built by Wendy
RAGLAN
Neck Rib

Place on Fold

Built by Wendy
RAGLAN
Waist Rib

Place on Fold

Built by Wendy
RAGLAN
Front

Place on Fold

Built by Wendy
RAGLAN
Back

Place on Fold

SEWING NOTES

For hems, you can also use your cover-stitch machine. If you don't have a serger to overlock the hem first, then leave the edge raw, fold back, and topstitch.

"stitch" = Use overlock or zigzag unless noted.

PATTERN PIECES

BUILT BY YOU
PROJECTS

Once again, these projects are just a sample of what you can create with the basic pattern. Feel free to mix and match the various details and techniques in each project to make your garment all your own.

Project #1:
A League of Your Own

I may be a lifelong long-suffering Cubs fan (maybe this will be their year! Hey, you never know), but you don't have to take this top out to the ball game. It's a boyishly attractive alternative to the basic T-shirt that looks great with jeans and mini-skirts and accentuates the wrists and forearms. Try a two-tone look, with different colors for sleeves and body, for an extra-sporty vibe. Or opt for a more sophisticated look in a soft lilac silk jersey with some soft gathers in the sleeve. You'll have two completely different styles from the same starting point.

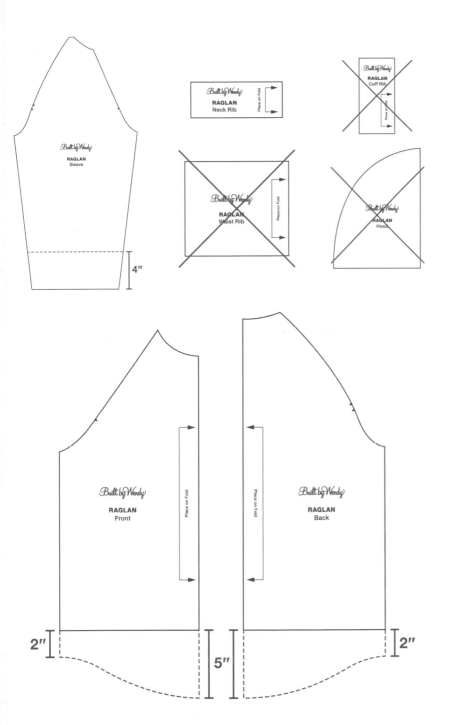

RAGLAN
Sleeve

4"

Built by Wendy
RAGLAN
Neck Rib
Place on Fold

Built by Wendy
RAGLAN
Cuff Rib
Place on Fold

Built by Wendy
RAGLAN
Waist Rib
Place on Fold

Built by Wendy
RAGLAN
Hood

Built by Wendy
RAGLAN
Front

Place on Fold

Place on Fold

Built by Wendy
RAGLAN
Back

2"

5"

2"

Supplies

1 yard jersey

1 yard contrast jersey

¼ yard rib (typically in the same color as the contrast jersey)

Pattern Adjustments

1. Shorten sleeves by 4″.

2. On the front and back body pieces, add 2″ at the side seams and 5″ at the center. Draw a new shaped hem.

CUTTING

Cut out the pattern pieces as shown.

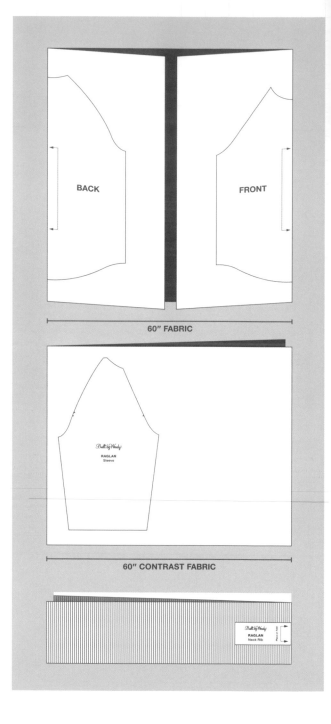

BACK

FRONT

60" FABRIC

Built by Wendy
RAGLAN
Sleeve

60" CONTRAST FABRIC

Built by Wendy
RAGLAN
Neck Rib

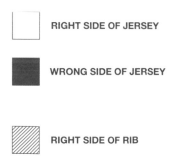

RIGHT SIDE OF JERSEY

WRONG SIDE OF JERSEY

RIGHT SIDE OF RIB

WRONG SIDE OF RIB

SEWING

1. With right sides together, stitch the front sleeves to the front armholes.

2. With right sides together, stitch the right back sleeve to the right back armhole.

3. With wrong sides together, fold the neck rib in half lengthwise. Stitch the raw edges of the neck rib to the neck opening, stretching the neck rib as you sew to fit it into larger neck opening.

4. With right sides together, stitch the left back sleeve to the left back armhole, including the neck rib.

5. With right sides together, stitch the front body to the back body along the side seams from the bottom up to the sleeve openings.

6. Overlock the raw edges of the bottom and sleeve openings, fold back, and topstitch (zigzag or cover-stitch).

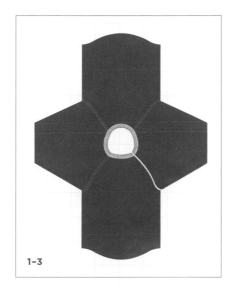

1-3

4

5

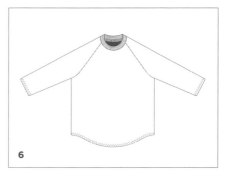

6

Project #2:
Flashdance Flashback

Who can forget the image of Jennifer Beals and her seductive, shoulder-revealing fleece top? It may once have been synonymous with the neo-retro '80s look, but in recent years this style has become a modern classic. It's comfy, it's sexy, and it hides a host of figure flaws. What's not to like?

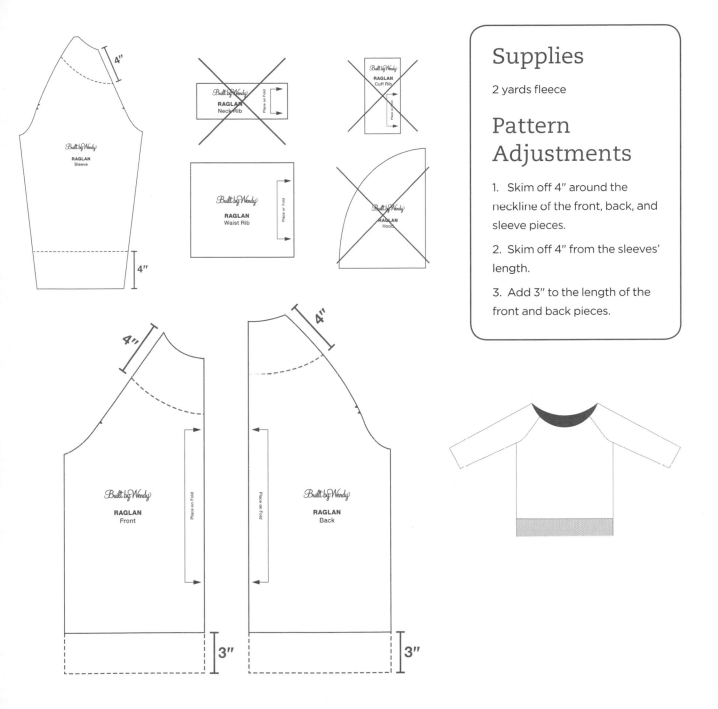

Supplies

2 yards fleece

Pattern Adjustments

1. Skim off 4" around the neckline of the front, back, and sleeve pieces.

2. Skim off 4" from the sleeves' length.

3. Add 3" to the length of the front and back pieces.

CUTTING

Cut out the pattern pieces shown.

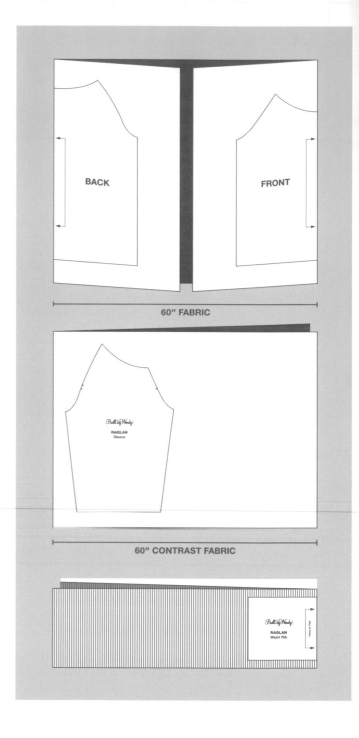

BACK

FRONT

60" FABRIC

RAGLAN
Sleeve

60" CONTRAST FABRIC

RAGLAN
Waist Rib

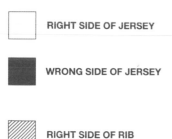

RIGHT SIDE OF JERSEY

WRONG SIDE OF JERSEY

RIGHT SIDE OF RIB

WRONG SIDE OF RIB

SEWING

1. With right sides together, stitch the front sleeves to the front armholes and the back sleeves to the back armholes.

2. With right sides together, stitch the front to the back at the right side from the bottom to the sleeve openings.

3. With wrong sides together, fold the waist rib in half lengthwise. Stitch the raw edges of the waist rib to the right side of the bottom opening, stretching as you sew to fit the rib into the larger bottom opening.

4. With right sides together, stitch the front body to the back body at the left side, from the bottom edge of the waist rib to the sleeve opening.

Note: You can keep the neck and sleeve openings raw, or you can overlook (or zigzag) them to create a more finished unfinished look, if you know what I mean!

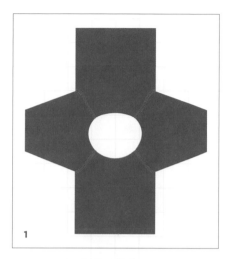

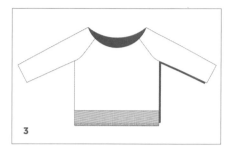

Project #3:
Halter Ego

Think of a halter as a raglan top
without the sleeves. This daring,
shoulder-baring silhouette can look
totally different depending on the
fabric you use. Try making one in
stretch silk under a blazer for a fancy
look, or in a jersey print for a breezy
summer top. The neck ties are a great
opportunity to get creative, too. Try
using contrasting or printed fabric, or
make a braid, or use upholstery rope
or anything else you can get your
hands on.

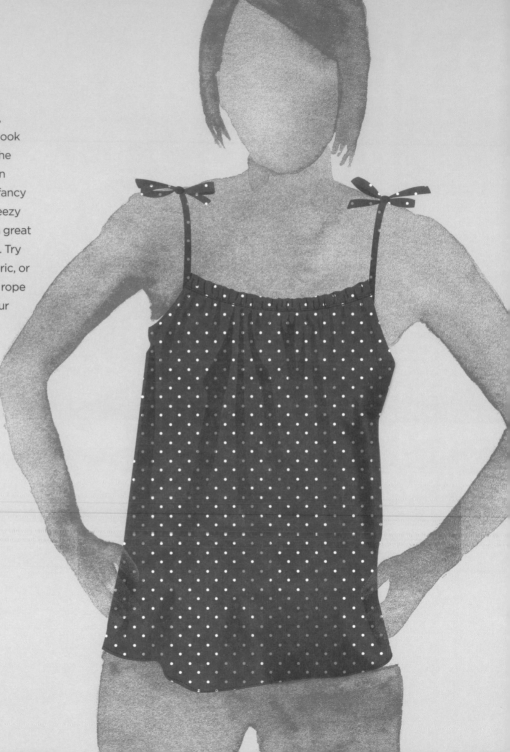

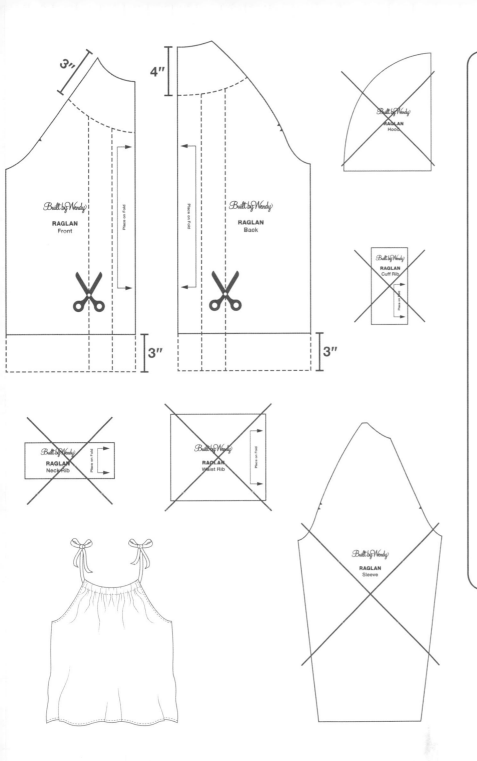

Supplies

1 yard jersey

1 1/2 yards ribbon, cord, or any other material you desire for the neck ties

Pattern Adjustments

1. Add 3″ to the length of the front and back pieces.

2. Remove 3″ from the front neckline.

3. Remove 4″ from the back neckline.

4. Make two vertical slash lines on the front and back pieces, as shown.

5. Cut along these lines and spread these pieces 2″ apart to make new pattern pieces. This will add a total of 4″ to each half pattern piece, for a total increase of 16″ around.

CUTTING

Cut out the pattern pieces as shown.

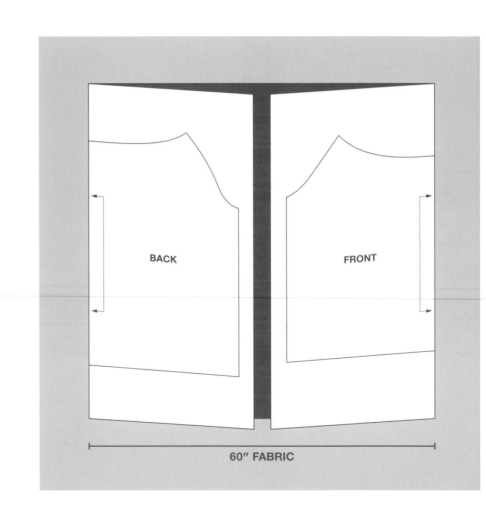

RIGHT SIDE OF JERSEY

WRONG SIDE OF JERSEY

BACK

FRONT

60" FABRIC

SEWING

1. With right sides together, stitch the front body to the back body along both sides.

2. Overlock the raw edges of the bottom opening, armholes, and top.

3. Fold back the bottom opening and armholes and topstitch (straight-stitch, zigzag, or cover-stitch).

4. Fold back the top edges 1″ and topstitch (straight-stitch). Fill this tube with cord, ribbon, or other neck tie material.

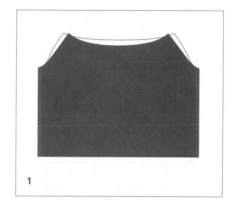

1

2, 3

4

Project #4:
A Peasant Surprise

Just how versatile is the raglan pattern? You can even use it to make this breezy, classic summer dress. Try adding a ruffle or decorative trim to the bottom, or use shiny stretch silk for a glamorous, cocktails-in-Capri vibe. Play around with the shoulder elastic length before you sew; as long as it's not too tight, you can switch between over-the-shoulder and sultry off-the-shoulder looks. However you spin this dress, it's bound to become one of your favorite outfits. Just throw on a belt, a necklace, and some sandals and you're good to go.

Supplies

3 yards jersey

1 yard ¼" elastic

Pattern Adjustments

1. Lower the front body neckline 4" at the center front point and 2" at the armholes. Draw a new neckline connecting these points, as shown.

2. Lower the back neckline 1" across.

3. Add 16" to the front and back body length.

4. Make two vertical slash lines down the entire length of the front and back pieces.

5. Remove 2" from the tops of the sleeve pieces at the front and 1" at the back to blend in with the new body neckline. Redraw the lines to match up with the new body pattern.

6. Remove 3" from the sleeves' length.

7. Make two vertical slash lines on the sleeves, as shown.

8. Slash and spread the front and back body pieces, adding 2" between each slash mark, for a total of 4" additional width on each half pattern piece. Do the same thing with the sleeves.

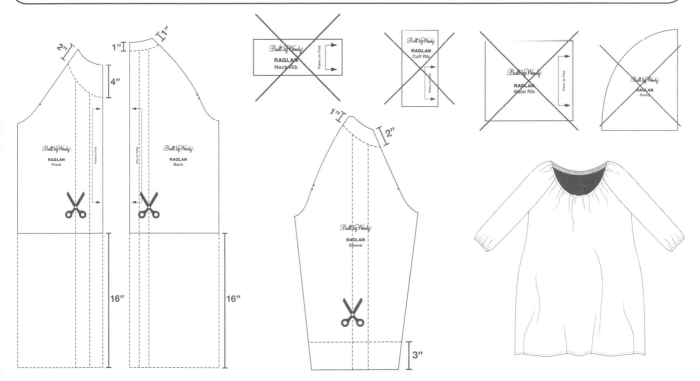

CUTTING

Cut out the pattern pieces as shown.

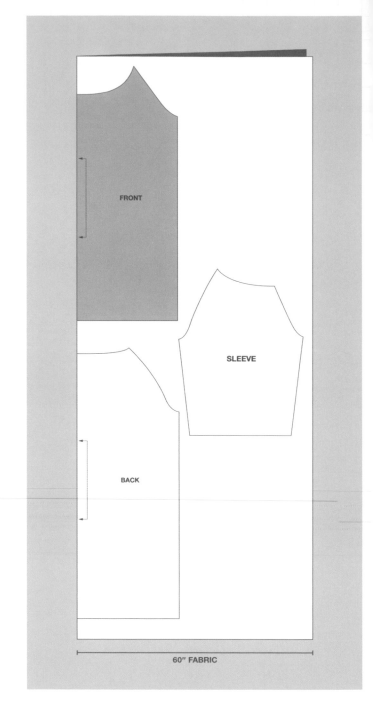

FRONT

SLEEVE

BACK

60" FABRIC

WRONG SIDE OF JERSEY

PATTERN PIECE FLIPPED

SEWING

1. With right sides together, stitch the front sleeves to the front armholes.

2. With right sides together, stitch the left back sleeve to the left back armhole.

3. Overlock the neck opening's raw edge, fold back ½", and topstitch (straight-stitch or zigzag). Fill this tube with elastic and pull so that it gathers to your liking (it's best to figure out exactly how much you want to use beforehand). Pin the elastic at each end opening so it doesn't pull through the tube before you anchor it with a seam.

4. Repeat these steps for the sleeve openings and elastic.

5. With right sides together, stitch the right back sleeve to the right back armhole. This seam will anchor the elastic (pull out pins while sewing).

6. With right sides together, stitch the front body to the back body along the side seams, from the bottom up to the sleeve openings (anchoring the elastic as you sew over it to create side seams).

7. Overlock the bottom opening, fold back 1", and topstitch (straight-stitch, zigzag, or cover- stitch).

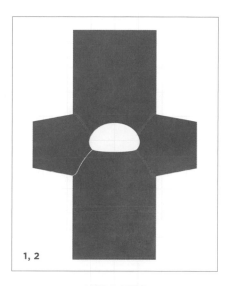

1, 2

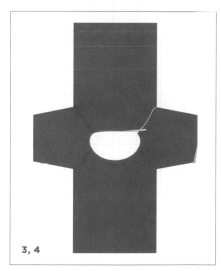

3, 4

5, 6

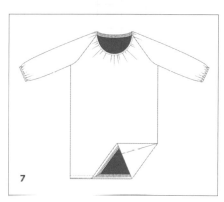

7

Project #5:
In the Hoodie

Not so long ago, the hoodie was
a garment reserved for gym class
and juvenile delinquents. Now it's
a staple of every chic downtown
girl's wardrobe and even has a Lady
Sovereign song named after it! A
hoodie is just the thing to toughen
up a dress or heels or layer under
a tailored jacket for extra warmth.
And, of course, you can take it to the
gym. My version of this classic shape
is streamlined for the female figure.
Try it in terry or fleece, and if you like,
make it oversize, add appliqués, or
mix up the trim color. This version uses
an unlined hood with no drawstring,
but you can add one or both of these
features if you want. Because this
style uses a zipper, it's slightly more
complicated than some of the other
patterns in this chapter, but it's still
fairly simple. Consult *Sew U* if you
need a complete guide to how to
sew a zipper.

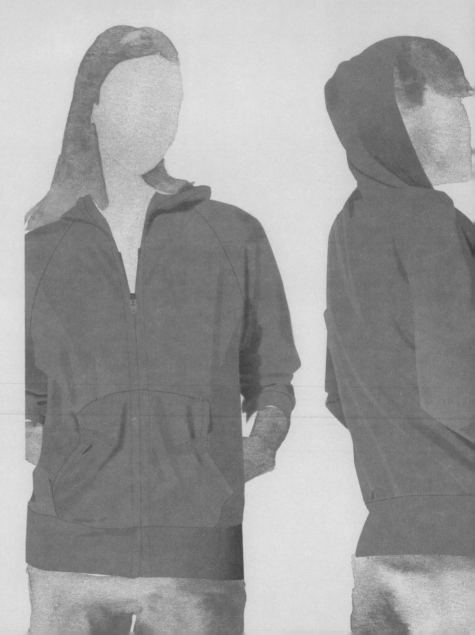

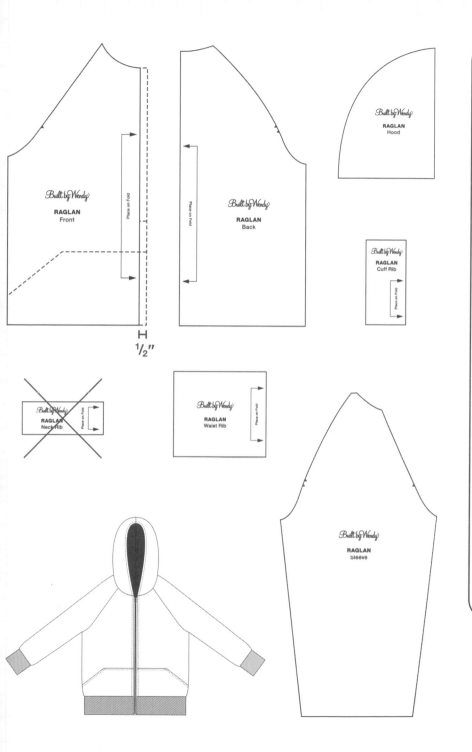

Supplies

2 yards fleece

½ yard rib

20″ separating zipper

Pattern Adjustments

1. Add ½″ seam allowance to the center front of the front pattern piece. The pattern piece is on the half, and normally you would place this half pattern on a fold. Since the garment will have a zipper down the front, you will not cut it on the fold. But you do need to add a ½″ seam allowance down the center front to sew the zipper there.

2. Trace the pocket shape as shown.

3. Transfer the pocket shapes to pattern paper. Add seam allowances and cut the new pieces.

CUTTING

Cut the pattern pieces as shown.
Note that the new front pattern piece
is not cut on the fold.

TIP

If you'd like a lined hood rather than one
whose wrong side shows when down (you
might want to do this if you're working with
sweatshirt fleece), here's how to do it. First
cut duplicates of the hood pieces. Place the
right and left hood pieces with right sides
together and stitch down the center. Do the
same with the hood lining pieces. Then, with
right sides together, stitch the hood lining
to the hood around the front. Fold over so
that the front is clean-edged. Pin the raw
edges of the hood and hood lining together
around the neckline. Stitch this to the right
side of the body neck opening, lining up the
center back and shoulder points.

☐ RIGHT SIDE OF JERSEY

■ WRONG SIDE OF JERSEY

▨ RIGHT SIDE OF RIB

▨ WRONG SIDE OF RIB

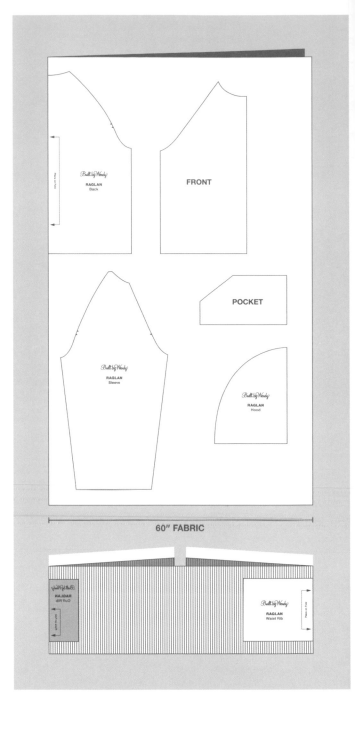

SEWING

1. Overlock the raw edge of the pocket opening, fold back ½", and topstitch (zigzag, straight-stitch, or cover-stitch). Then fold back the top edge of the pocket by ½" and pin it to the front body.

2. Topstitch (straight-stitch) the top edge of the pocket, removing pins as you sew. Pin the pocket sides to the body side seams (you will anchor these into seams when you sew the side seams later).

3. With right sides together, stitch the sleeves to the front and back armholes.

4. With wrong sides together, fold the cuff rib in half lengthwise. Stitch the raw edges of the cuff rib to the right side of the sleeve opening.

5. With right sides together, stitch the front body to the back body along the side seams, from the bottom opening up to the cuff opening.

6. With wrong sides together, fold the waist rib in half lengthwise. Stitch the raw edge of the waist rib to the right side of the bottom opening, stretching as you sew so that the rib fits into the larger bottom opening.

7. With right sides together, stitch the left and right hood pieces down the center.

8. With right sides together, stitch the hood neckline to the neck opening, matching the center hood seam to the center back and the hood's front edges to the body's front edges.

9. Overlock the raw edges of the center front opening, from the waist rib up all the way around the hood opening and back down to the other front waist rib.

10. Fold back the edges of the body opening by ½". Slip zipper tape underneath, placing it so that the top zipper pull is ½" below the hood neck seam. Topstitch (straight-stitch) so that you are sewing the zipper to the body and creating a clean edge. Continue hemming the hood as you sew around the entire opening, and go back down the other side of the zippered opening as you did with the first side of the zipper.

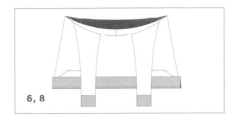

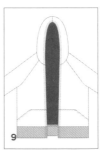

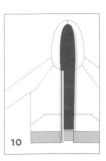

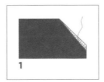

Project #6:
Life's a Beach

Sure, you can get away with throwing
on a tank and shorts for a day at the
beach, but this easy, swingy terry dress
is so much more fun, and it absorbs
water to boot. Try making yours
in a colorful print to maximize the
'60s-pop-star-on-holiday-in-Hawaii
effect. (Or, if you like the shape, try
making it in bright silk jersey—just
don't expect it to help with the wet-
swimsuit situation.)

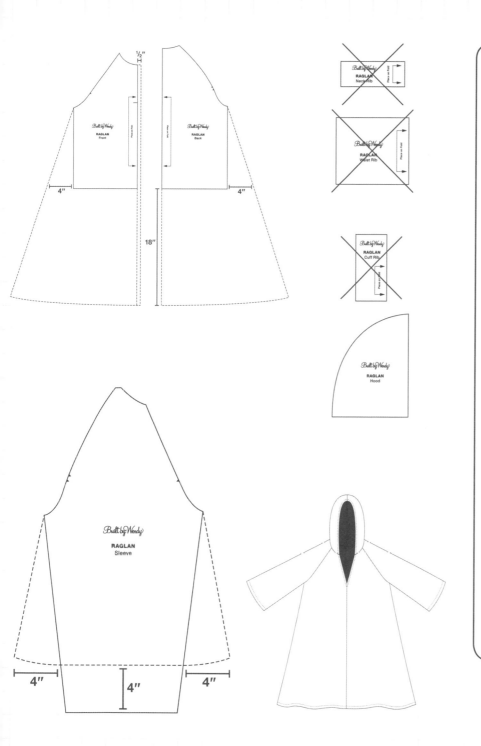

Supplies

3 yards printed terry

Pattern Adjustments

1. On the front and back, make a mark 4″ out from the side seam at the hem.

2. Draw a new side seam from the underarm to this point, and continue down at the same angle for 18″.

3. Add 18″ to the hem length at the center.

4. Connect the dots to make a new hem, curving up a little at the side seam so that the hem and side seam meet at a 90-degree angle.

5. Add ½″ seam allowance to the center front.

6. Shorten the sleeves by 4″.

7. To create flared sleeves, start 4″ out from the side seam at the new, shorter sleeve opening and draw a line up to the underarm of the sleeve.

CUTTING

Cut out the pattern pieces as shown.

RIGHT SIDE OF JERSEY

WRONG SIDE OF JERSEY

PATTERN PIECE FLIPPED

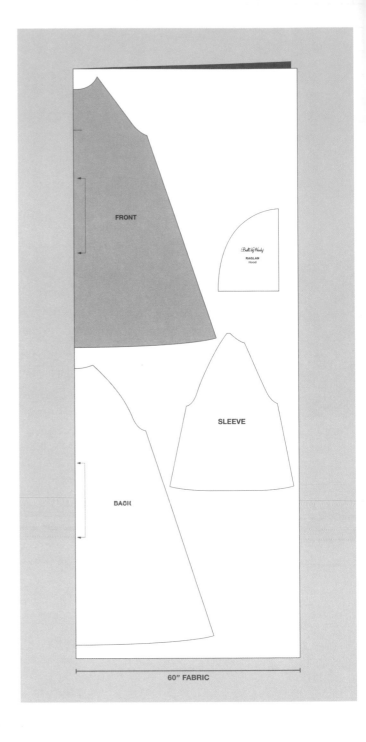

FRONT

RAGLAN
Hood

SLEEVE

BACK

60" FABRIC

SEWING

1. With right sides together, stitch the sleeves to the front and back armholes.

2. Overlock the raw edges of the sleeve openings.

3. With right sides together, stitch the front body to the back body along the side seams, from the bottom up to the sleeve openings.

4. Fold back the sleeve openings 1″ and topstitch (straight-stitch).

5. With right sides together, stitch the left and right hood pieces together down the center seam. If you want the hood lined, then cut another hood set, stitch the center seam, and with right sides together, stitch the hood and hood lining together around the front edge. Turn this inside out so the front edge is clean and the hood is completely lined.

6. With right sides together, stitch the hood neckline to the body neck opening. If the hood is lined, then start stitching the hood ½″ in from the center front seam allowance.

7. Overlock the bottom opening and the front raw edge all the way around the hood. (If your hood is lined, then overlock the front raw edge to the top of the front.)

8. With right sides together, stitch the center fronts together from the bottom opening up to the center front notch. Press the seam open flat, folding back the seam allowance between the notch and the top edge where the hood is attached.

9. Topstitch (straight-stitch) this center front neck opening.

1, 2

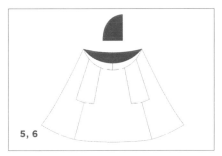

5, 6

8

3, 4

7

9

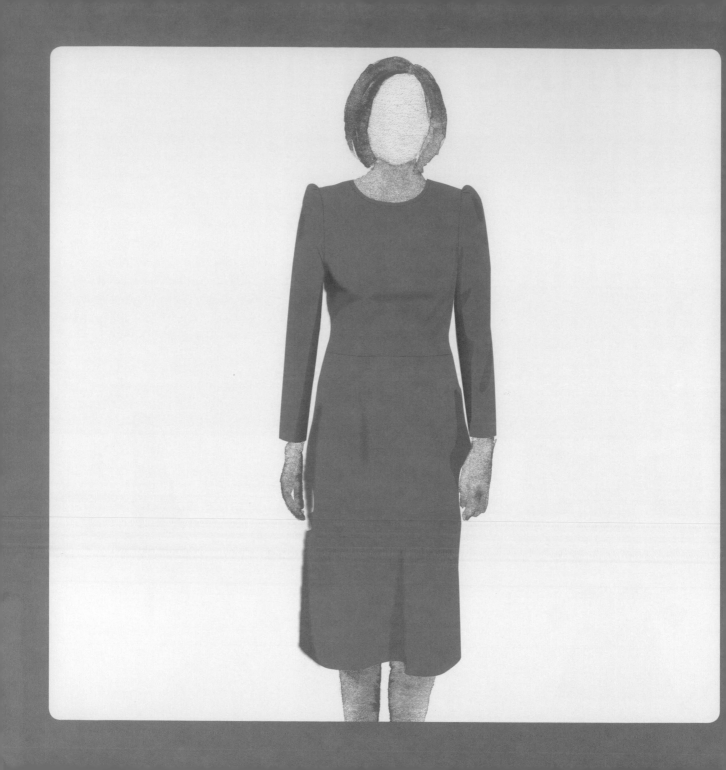

CHAPTER 9
DRESSES AND KNITS

Taking Knits to the Next Level

A DRESS MADE OF KNIT FABRIC IS PRETTY MUCH THE PERFECT GARMENT. YOU CAN STRETCH OUT IN IT, CURL UP IN IT, AND TAKE TWELVE-HOUR PLANE RIDES IN IT.

You can toss it in your tote bag for a quick change later in the day, and you'll still look feminine and polished when you throw it on. You can wear it with heels for a big night out or scruff it up with Chucks for pizza and a DVD at your boyfriend's place. Why wouldn't you want to own multiple versions?

The great news is that with the simple pattern included in this book, you can. My dress pattern has two body parts—the bodice and the skirt—which multiplies the options for customizing exponentially. You can take the skirt from one project and use it with the bodice of another and play around with the length and width of both. For instance, why not try a drop-waist minidress with a long bodice and a tiny skirt? As you can with the patterns in the other chapters, you may choose to remove sleeves, add hoods and pockets, and make hems shorter or longer. Plus each dress idea in this chapter can also be made into a shirt, if you leave off the skirt part. The possibilities are so vast, you may never want to go shopping for store-bought clothes again! (Well, just kidding. Sort of.)

DRESS
Waistband

DRESS
Bodice Back

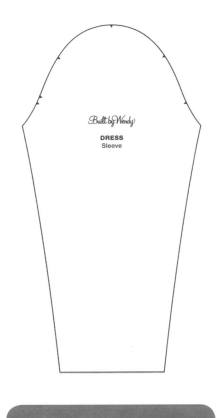

DRESS
Sleeve

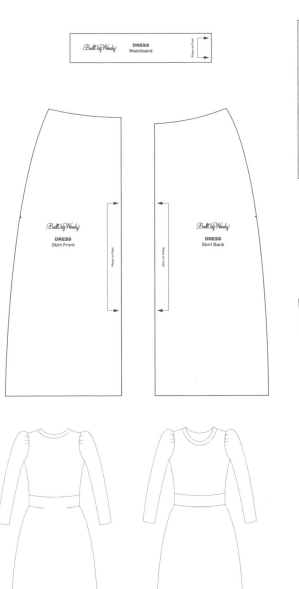

DRESS
Skirt Front

DRESS
Skirt Back

DRESS
Bodice Front

SEWING NOTES

For hems, you can also use your cover-stitch machine. If you don't have a serger to overlock the hem first, then leave the edge raw, fold back, and topstitch.

"stitch" = Use overlock or zigzag unless noted.

PATTERN PIECES

BUILT BY YOU
PROJECTS

As discussed, the sky's the limit
when it comes to designing a dress.
Think of these projects as the first of
many options you can explore, and
let your imagination run wild. Try
mixing and matching necklines, bodices, skirts, and sleeves from these
projects and adding pockets, trim,
and any other good-looking detail
you can dream up. The skirt part of
the pattern can also be used alone
to make all sorts of skirts. *Sew U* has
a variety of suggestions for customizing that will come in handy here.

Project #1:
Yacht to Trot

Whether you've scored an invite to an afternoon boat cruise in the Hamptons or simply want something chic and simple for kicking around town, this crisp, classic look will never let you down. Feel free to add quirky trims or buttons and mess around with skirt and sleeve lengths.

WAISTBAND

SKIRT FRONT

SKIRT BACK

16"

2"

2"

SLEEVE

1"

1"

BODICE FRONT

BODICE BACK

Supplies

½ yard striped jersey

1 ¼ yards solid jersey

Pattern Adjustments

1. Skim off 16" from sleeves (or make them your desired length; this dress would be great with a three-quarter-length sleeve).

2. Skim off 2" from the length of the front and the back for the look shown here. (Again, it's your choice—this dress is also super-cute as a mini.)

3. Make the shoulders 1" wide.

4. Redraw the neckline to meet the new shoulders.

5. Make the neck binding piece 1" by 15" and cut on the fold.

CUTTING

Cut out the pattern pieces as shown
and cut the neck binding piece.

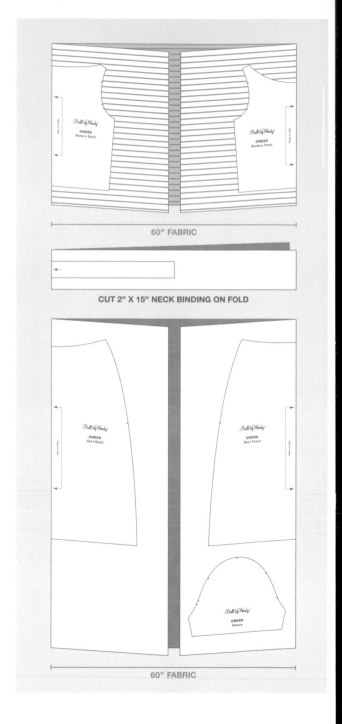

60" FABRIC

CUT 2" X 15" NECK BINDING ON FOLD

60" FABRIC

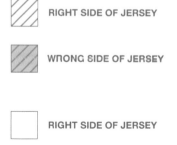

RIGHT SIDE OF JERSEY

WRONG SIDE OF JERSEY

RIGHT SIDE OF JERSEY

WRONG SIDE OF JERSEY

SEWING

1. With right sides together, stitch the front and back bodice pieces together at the left shoulder.

2. Stitch the binding around the neck. For this style I chose a mock bind with a lip, folded and topstitched along the rib edge with a straight stitch. Since this neck is wide, you won't need to stretch the binding out as you sew.

3. With right sides together, stitch the front and back bodice pieces together at the right shoulder.

4. Gather the sleeve caps.

5. With right sides together, stitch the sleeves to the armholes. Overlock each sleeve opening.

6. With right sides together, stitch the front skirt to the front bodice at the waist. Do the same for the back.

7. With right sides together, stitch the front body to the back body along the side seam, from the bottom up to the sleeve openings.

8. Overlock the bottom hem, fold back 1″, and topstitch. Use a regular straight stitch, since you won't be stretching the hem much.

9. Fold back each sleeve opening and topstitch. This time use a zigzag stitch, since this sleeve is fitted and will need to stretch.

1

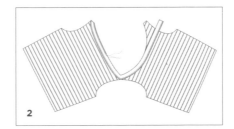

4

2

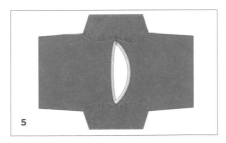

3

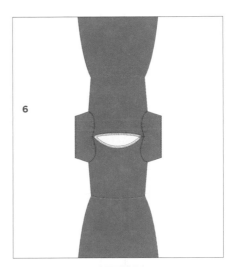

6

7

8, 9

Project #2:
Belle de Jour

This minidress is rendered slightly
more modest by its long sleeves
and crewneck. It has a very '60s feel,
especially if you make it in a dark wool
jersey, as suggested. Why not play
up that vibe and make a matching
headband out of the same fabric?
Because the dress is so simple, it's a
great canvas to show off a good piece
of jewelry, like Grandma's vintage
brooch or a big, glittering necklace.
You can always skip the belt and
tie a pretty scarf or unique ribbon
around your waist. Or, if you like the
shape but want a more casual, warm-
weather feel, try making the dress in
lightweight cotton jersey.

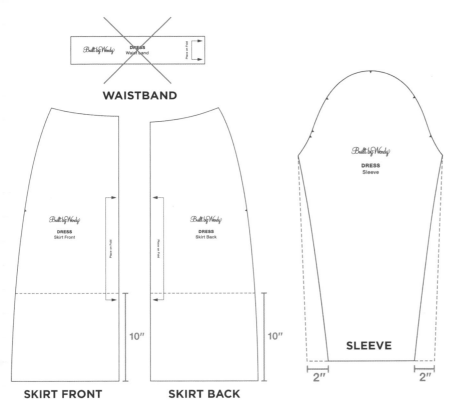

WAISTBAND

SKIRT FRONT

10"

SKIRT BACK

10"

DRESS
Sleeve

SLEEVE

2"   2"

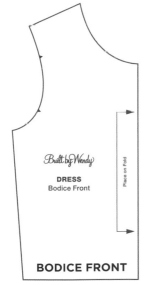

BODICE FRONT

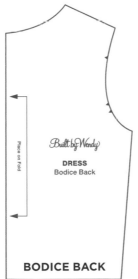

DRESS
Bodice Back

BODICE BACK

Supplies

2 yards wool jersey

1 yard 4" elastic

Pattern Adjustments

1. Add 2" to the sleeve side seams at the sleeve opening. Blend this new width as shown up to underarms.

2. Shorten the front and back skirt pieces 10".

3. Make a belt pattern piece measuring 4" by 20". Cut on the fold.

4. Make a neck binding piece measuring 1" by 8". Cut on the fold.

CUTTING

Cut out the pattern pieces as
shown, including neck binding and
belt pieces.

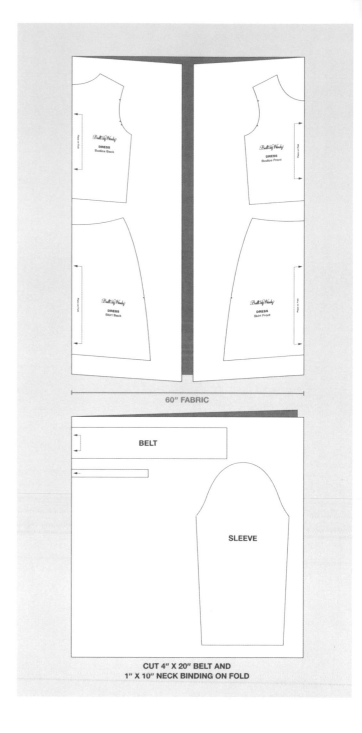

60" FABRIC

BELT

SLEEVE

CUT 4" X 20" BELT AND
1" X 10" NECK BINDING ON FOLD

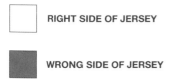

RIGHT SIDE OF JERSEY

WRONG SIDE OF JERSEY

SEWING

1. With right sides together, stitch the front and back bodice pieces together at the left shoulder.

2. Sew the binding around the neckline. For this example, I chose a mock bind. Topstitch along the edge using a zigzag stitch; because this neck is tight, it needs to stretch.

3. With right sides together, stitch the front and back bodice pieces together at the right shoulder.

4. Gather the sleeve caps. With right sides together, stitch the sleeves to the armholes.

5. Cut a piece of elastic about three quarters of the sleeve hem length. Overlock (zigzag if you have a conventional machine) the elastic onto the wrong side of the sleeve opening, pulling the elastic as you sew so you are gathering the fabric into the elastic.

6. With right sides together, stitch the front bodice to the front skirt at the waist. Repeat the step for the back pieces.

7. With right sides together, stitch the front body to the back body along the side seam, from the bottom up to the sleeve openings.

8. Overlock the bottom opening, fold back 1", and sew, using a zigzag topstitch to allow for some stretching.

9. Fold back each sleeve opening (thus encasing the elastic in the hem) and run a zigzag stitch to allow for stretch, pulling the hem flat as you sew.

10. If you're making the belt, fold the belt piece in half lengthwise, right sides together. Overlock the edges together. Turn the tube inside out, fold in the raw edges at each end by about ½", and topstitch.

Project #3:
Pretty Baby-doll

No dress hides figure flaws better than this one. It's flattering and comfortable, and has a romantic air about it—especially in a festive floral print like this one.

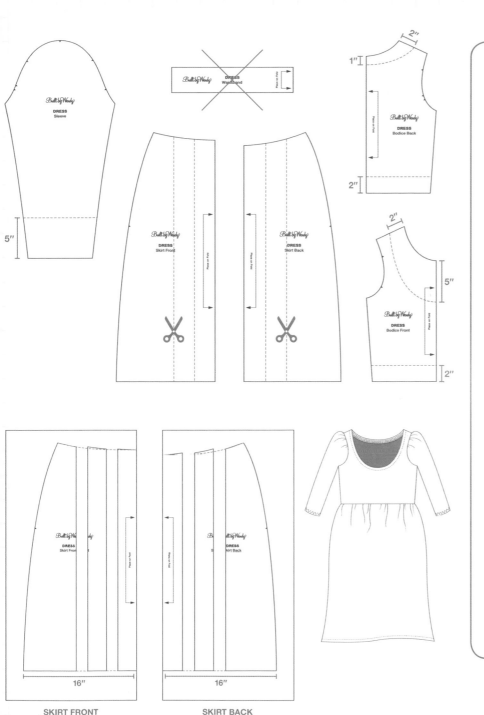

Supplies

2 yards cotton/Lycra blend jersey

1 yard ¼" elastic

Pattern Adjustments

1. Shorten sleeves 5".

2. On the back neckline, trim off 1" from the center back neck point and 2" from the neck at the shoulders. Blend to draw a new neckline, as shown. Shorten bodice 2".

3. On the front neckline, trim off 5" at the center front neck point and 2" from the neck at the shoulders. Blend to draw a new neckline, as shown. Shorten bodice 2".

4. Make two vertical slash lines from top to bottom of both the front and the back skirt pattern.

5. Spread the front and back skirt pattern pieces so they are each 16" wide.

SKIRT FRONT

SKIRT BACK

CUTTING

Cut out the pattern pieces as shown.

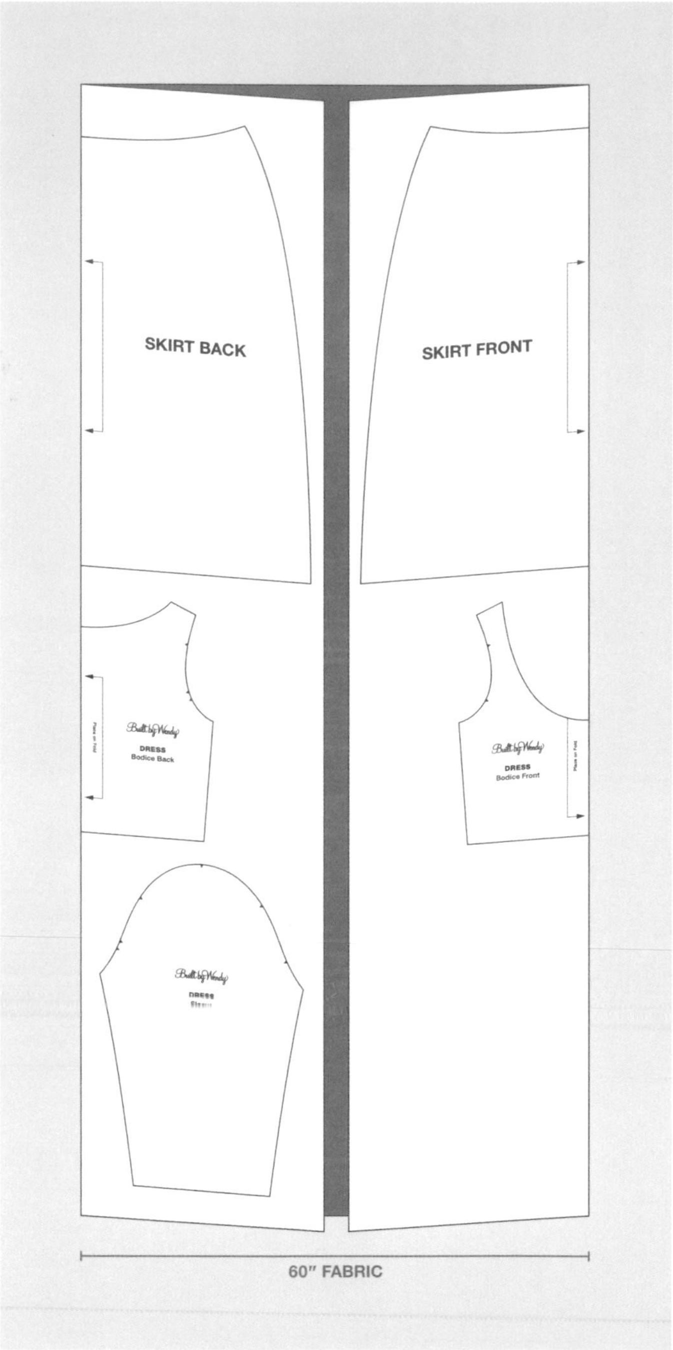

SKIRT BACK

SKIRT FRONT

Built by Wendy
DRESS
Bodice Back

Built by Wendy
DRESS
Bodice Front

Built by Wendy
DRESS
Sleeve

60" FABRIC

☐ **RIGHT SIDE OF JERSEY**

■ **WRONG SIDE OF JERSEY**

SEWING

1. With right sides together, stitch the front and back bodice pieces together at the left shoulder.

2. Overlock (or zigzag if you have a conventional machine) elastic to the wrong side of the neck opening. Do not pull; just sew it flat.

3. With right sides together, stitch the front and back bodice pieces together at the left shoulder.

4. Gather the sleeve caps.

5. With right sides together, stitch the sleeves to the armholes. Overlock the sleeve openings.

6. Gather the skirt front along the top edge (the waist's raw edge). With right sides together, stitch the gathered skirt waist edge to the bodice waist edge.

7. Do the same for the back.

8. With right sides together, stitch the front body to the back body along the side seam, from the bottom up to the sleeve openings.

9. Overlock the bottom hem, fold back 1", and topstitch with a straight stitch (no stretch necessary).

10. Fold back each sleeve opening $\frac{1}{2}$" and run a zigzag topstitch to allow for stretch.

11. Fold back the neck opening so the elastic is encased inside the seam. Run a straight topstitch around the hem.

8

1

6, 7

9, 10

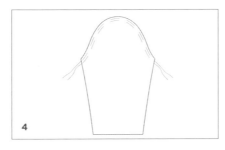

4

5

11

3

Project #4:
Madame Butterfly

This ethereal shape drapes beautifully—and feels divine against your skin—when you make it out of silk jersey. With its deep V-neck, billowing elbow-length angel sleeves, and ruffled hem, it's a sexy and festive addition to your wardrobe. Because it has facings, it's a slightly more complicated pattern to make, but it will prove well worth the extra effort when you step out of the house looking like a heavenly creature.

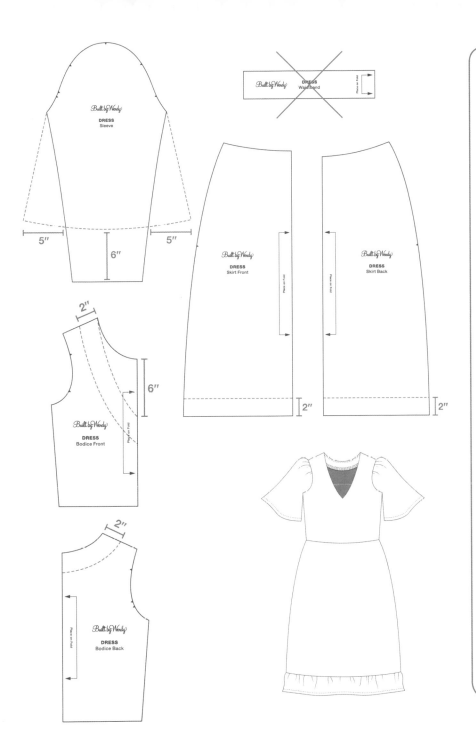

Supplies

2 yards silk jersey

1 yard ¼" elastic

½" fusible interfacing

Pattern Adjustments

1. Shorten sleeves 6". Add 5" to each side seam at the new shortened length and blend the new side seam up to the armhole.

2. Trace 2" around the back bodice neck opening. Transfer this shape as "back facing."

3. Drop the center front of the front bodice 6". Blend this V-neckline shape up to the shoulders.

4. Trace 2" around the front bodice's new V-shaped neckline. Transfer this shape as "front facing."

5. Shorten the front and back skirt pieces by 2".

6. Make a ruffle piece measuring 4" by 18". Cut on the fold.

CUTTING

Cut out the pattern pieces as shown, including the facings and the ruffle piece.

☐ **RIGHT SIDE OF JERSEY**

■ **WRONG SIDE OF JERSEY**

☐ **RIGHT SIDE OF FUSIBLE**

■ **WRONG SIDE OF FUSIBLE**

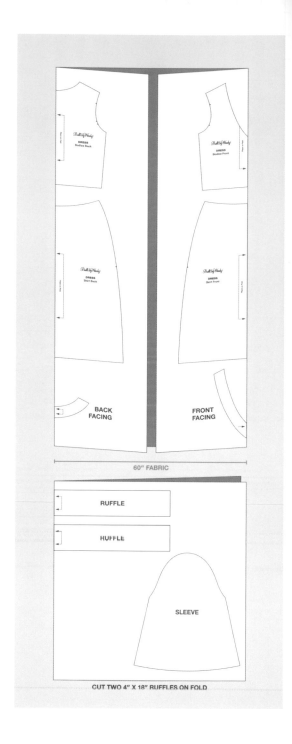

60" FABRIC

CUT TWO 4" X 18" RUFFLES ON FOLD

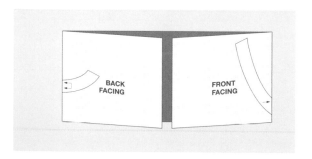

SEWING

1. With right sides together, stitch the front bodice to the back bodice at the shoulders.

2. Iron fusible interfacing to the wrong side of the front and back facing pieces. With right sides together, stitch the front and back facing pieces together at the shoulders. Overlock the entire outer edge of the facing.

3. With right sides together, stitch the facing to the neck opening's raw edge.

4. Turn the facing to the inside and press the seam toward the facing. Understitch the seam to the facing using your conventional machine. Tack the facing edge to the insides of the shoulder seams, as shown, using a hand needle and thread.

5. Gather the sleeve caps.

6. With right sides together, stitch the sleeves to the armholes.

7. With right sides together, stitch the front bodice to the front skirt at the waist. Do the same for the back.

8. With right sides together, stitch the front body to the back body along the side seam, from the bottom up to the sleeve opening.

9. Overlock each sleeve opening. Fold back ½" and topstitch with a straight stitch.

10. With right sides together, stitch the ruffle pieces together at their side seams.

11. To hem the ruffle, overlock one edge of the ruffle. Fold back ½" and topstitch with a straight stitch.

12. To turn it into a ruffle, gather the raw edge. With right sides together, pin the ruffle's raw edge to the skirt's bottom opening. Evenly space the gathering so that it fits smoothly into the skirt's bottom opening. Stitch the pieces together, removing pins as you sew.

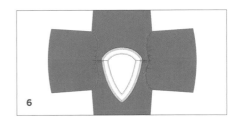

6

7

8 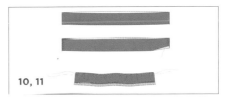 9

10, 11

1

2

3

4

5

12

Project #5:
Sweet Suspender

This jaunty look is one of my all-time
favorites. The slim-fitting skirt works
well in a cotton/Lycra blend for the
warmer months, or you might try
making yours in a cozy wool jersey for
winter and wear it with a turtleneck,
tights, and boots. If you prefer, you
can leave off the suspenders to make
a more sophisticated simple pencil
skirt. Feel free to play around with
contrasting accent pieces and buttons.
You might try making the suspenders
and waistband in a contrasting color
and add gold buttons for a sharp,
collegiate feeling. Or make the entire
thing in black with white buttons for
a New Wave look. You might even try
using animal- or heart-shaped buttons
from the flea market. Don't be afraid to
get creative!

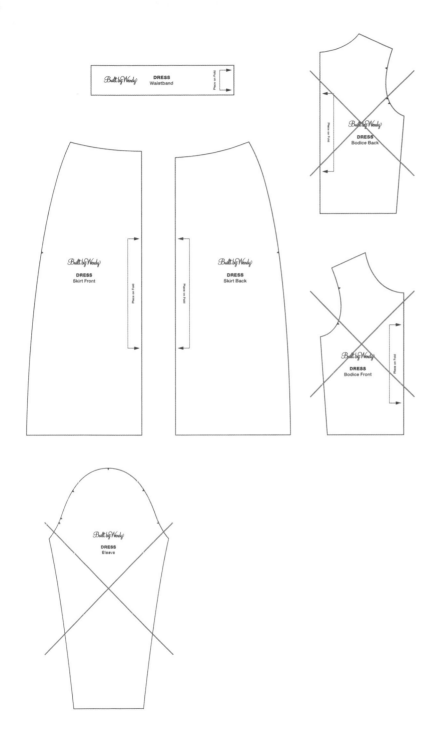

Built by Wendy
DRESS
Waistband

Built by Wendy
DRESS
Bodice Back

Built by Wendy
DRESS
Skirt Front

Built by Wendy
DRESS
Skirt Back

Built by Wendy
DRESS
Bodice Front

Built by Wendy
DRESS
Sleeve

Supplies

1 ½ yards jersey

1 yard 1″ elastic

¼ yard fusible interfacing

4 buttons

Pattern Adjustments

1. Make a suspender pattern piece measuring 3″ by 19″ on the fold.

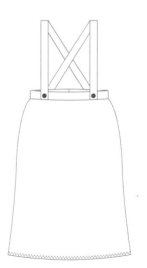

CUTTING

Cut out the pattern pieces as shown,
including the suspender piece.

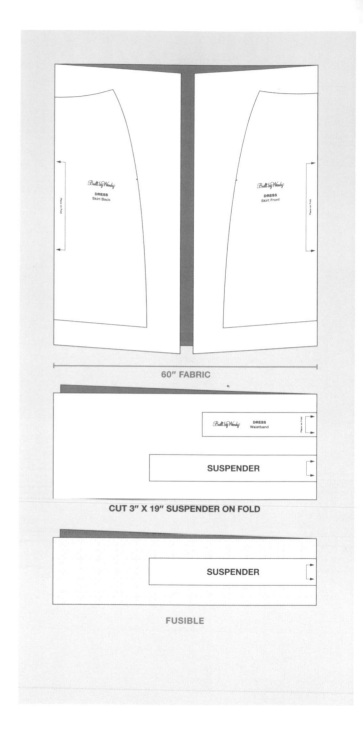

60" FABRIC

CUT 3" X 19" SUSPENDER ON FOLD

FUSIBLE

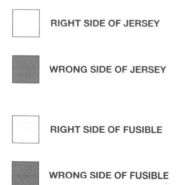

RIGHT SIDE OF JERSEY

WRONG SIDE OF JERSEY

RIGHT SIDE OF FUSIBLE

WRONG SIDE OF FUSIBLE

SEWING

1. With right sides together, stitch the front skirt piece to the back skirt piece along the side seams.

2. Overlock the hem, fold back 1", and run a zigzag topstitch to allow for stretch.

3. Fold the waistband piece in half crosswise, right sides together, and stitch the ends together along the raw edge to form a loop.

4. Cut the elastic into the same length as the waistband. Place one end on top of the other to form a loop, so that the ends cross over by 1/4". Stitch together to make a flat seam.

5. Fold the waistband in half lengthwise so that you are encasing the seam inside, and press to sharpen the fold. Slip the elastic loop inside the waistband fold and push it toward the fold's top edge, so you have a loose-floating elastic loop inside the waistband.

6. Stitch the raw edge of the waist-band to the top raw edge of the skirt's right side.

7. Iron fusible interfacing to the wrong side of each suspender piece. Fold each piece in half lengthwise, right sides together, and stitch the raw edges together.

8. Turn the tube inside out, fold in the ends by 1/2", and topstitch them closed.

9. Attach each suspender end to the waistband (place each about 3" or 4" from the center front) by hand, stitching a button through the suspenders and waistband. (For the definitive guide to button-sewing, consult *Sew U*.) Crisscross the straps in back and attach with a button.

6

1, 2

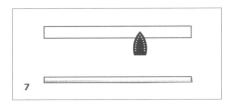
8

3

7

4

5

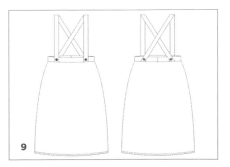
9

Project #6:
Tiny Bubble

Who knew you could make a strapless dress from a pattern with sleeves? With a few adjustments, it's easy. This flirty strapless style is an urban classic: The blouson shape is flattering and flaw-concealing, while the gathers nicely hide a strapless bra. The flat waistband's contrast with the gathered top and bottom creates an hourglass figure. Try covering up with a favorite cardigan, or wear the dress solo in the summer with sandals and shades.

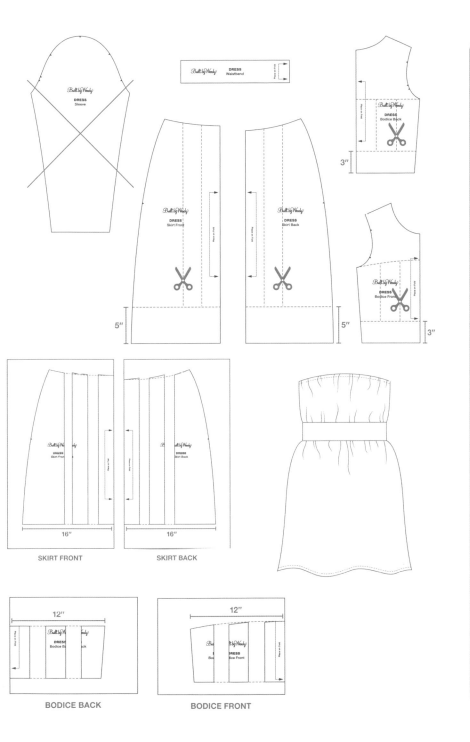

SKIRT FRONT

SKIRT BACK

BODICE BACK

BODICE FRONT

Supplies

1 ½ yards jersey

1 yard ½" elastic

Pattern Adjustments

1. Shorten the front and back bodice pieces by 3".

2. On the back bodice, draw a straight horizontal line from under the armhole at the side seam to the center back.

3. On the front bodice, draw a curved line from under the armhole at the side seam to the center front.

4. Make two vertical slash lines down the entire front and back bodices.

5. Shorten the front and back skirt pieces by 5".

6. Make two vertical slash lines down the entire front and back skirt pattern pieces.

7. Spread the front and back bodices so that they are each 12" wide.

8. Spread the front and back skirts so that they are 16" wide.

CUTTING

Cut out the pattern pieces as shown.

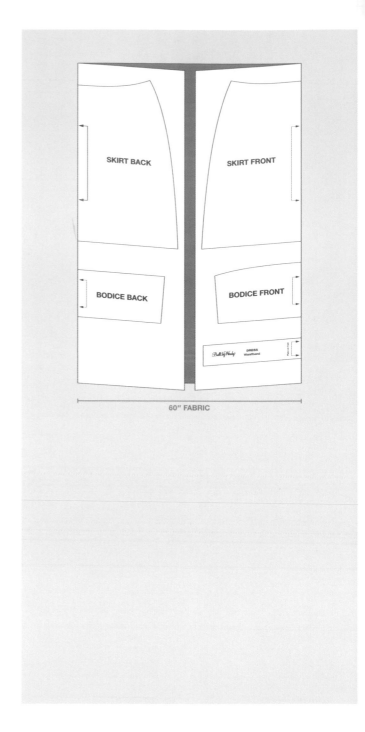

SKIRT BACK

SKIRT FRONT

BODICE BACK

BODICE FRONT

60" FABRIC

RIGHT SIDE OF JERSEY

WRONG SIDE OF JERSEY

SEWING

1. With right sides together, stitch the front bodice to the back bodice at the left side.

2. With right sides together, stitch the front skirt to the back skirt at the left side.

3. Gather the bottom edge of the bodice (front and back).

4. Overlock the top edge of the bodice, fold it back ³⁄₄″, and topstitch with a straight stitch. Fill the tube with ¹⁄₂″ elastic. (Wrap the elastic around your chest above your bust first. Cut a length that is comfortable and snug—you don't want to flash anybody.) Secure the elastic at each end with a pin; it will be anchored by a side seam later.

5. Gather the top edge of the skirt (front and back).

6. With right sides together, stitch the waistband to the skirt's gathered edge. You might want to pin this first and adjust the gathers so they fit into the waistband's length.

7. With right sides together, stitch the waistband to the bodice's gathered edge. Pin this first as well, and adjust the gathers to fit into the waistband's length.

8. With right sides together, stitch the front body to the back body along the right side seam. Overlock the bottom opening, fold it back 1″, and topstitch using a straight stitch.

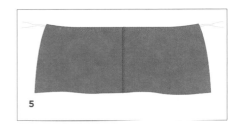

5

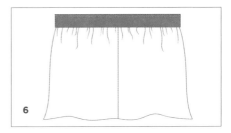

6

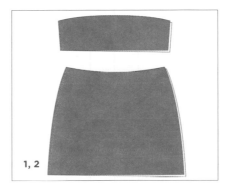

1, 2

7

3, 4

8

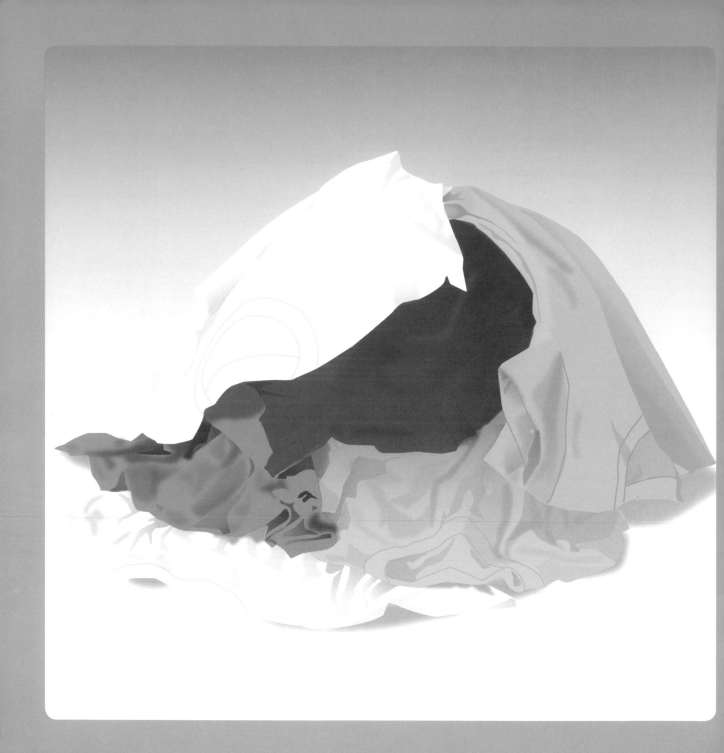

CHAPTER 10
RECYCLING

Giving Old Knits a New Lease on Life

AS THE SAYING GOES, ONE MAN'S TRASH IS ANOTHER MAN'S TREASURE. IN SEWING, ONE WOMAN'S TRASH CAN BECOME THAT SAME WOMAN'S TREASURE!

A great way—and a very cheap way—to get comfortable with sewing stretch fabric is to remake or alter the knit clothing you already have. Sure, we all have our Salvation Army pile of too-small or worn-out T-shirts and sweatshirts. But what may seem like a bunch of old rags is actually a very valuable source of knit fabric and a perfect opportunity to flex your creative muscles. Plus the tips in this chapter will come in handy the next time you're at a thrift store and stumble across something with great fabric and a hideous shape (haven't we all experienced that before?). If nothing else, these projects will make for great technical practice for sewing original garments. But hey, you never know what future masterpieces may lurk in the dark recesses of your basement! Here are some of my favorite ideas for how to bring your unwanted rugby shirts, polo shirts, T-shirts, sweatshirts, and thermals—and even swimsuits—back from the dead.

In the same way that you lay your pattern on top of a yard of fabric and cut it out, you can think of oversize men's T-shirts and sweatshirts as a large canvas from which to form your new garment. If the garment isn't that big and you don't have enough fabric for your new garment, you can always combine a couple of T-shirts for a new look. Simply rip open the seams or cut just outside the seams, whichever is easier. Fold each garment piece in half as you would a piece of new fabric, lay the pattern pieces on top, and cut them out.

LOVE WILL TEAR US APART
USING OLD GARMENTS AS FABRIC

GRAPHIC MATERIAL
SILKSCREENS

I tend to hang on to things for sentimental reasons—especially T-shirts. It's hard to throw that stuff away. Chances are you have some great tees with silkscreens you love, whether they're old concert shirts or vacation memorabilia. But maybe you don't want to wear that Cancun tank top ten years after your last spring break.

What to Do?

Consider using the silkscreen as an **appliqué**. Just cut it around the edges, iron some fusible interfacing onto the back to stabilize it, pin it to the face of a new garment, and zigzag it on.

Another idea (and a great cheap gift) is to cut out the silkscreen and make it into a pillow or stuffed animal. It's easy: Simply cut around the shape through the front and the back of the shirt, leaving a seam allowance around the edge. Turn the pieces so they're face to face and stitch around the edge, leaving a few inches open. Turn it inside out and fill it with stuffing (also

called bunting, and available at fabric stores) or simply pull the stuffing out of an old pillow. You can even close it shut with a few hand stitches or small safety pins for a punked-out Stephen Sprouse look.

PATCH PERFECT

Try combining different garments to make one. For starters, you can take two T-shirts, cut each one straight down the middle, and sew one half of each shirt to one half of the other. Now you have two new shirts! This might not be the look for you, but it's an interesting exercise in creativity. You can go on and on, cutting apart garments and attaching pieces together. I love to take a few tees, cut horizontal slashes through them, and reattach them to create patchwork stripes. You might try diamond shapes, curved shapes, vertical lines, checkerboard grids...the possibilities are endless.

If you have a serger, you can have a ton of fun with too-big garments. Simply turn the item inside out and serge the side seams. Try it on, and if it's still too big, serge some more off. (You can also use this technique with a conventional machine, of course—simply use a zigzag stitch and trim off the excess.)

Another way to change the shape of a garment is to add elastic at sleeve hems to make puff or poet sleeves, and at bottom hems to make bubble skirts. Do both to create a feminine, body-conscious tunic from a slouchy men's tee.

SLIM FAST
ALTERING FIT

PARTS AND LABOR
MIXING AND MATCHING DIFFERENT GARMENTS

Why not use parts of old garments and combine them with new pieces? You might take an old one-piece bathing suit, cut off the bottom half at the waistline, and attach a dirndl-style gathered skirt of layered lace. You can do the same thing with those great old polyester slips with lace insets—they're sold at almost any flea market, in case you don't have your own. Or create an Empire-waist baby-doll dress by cutting off an old, tight T-shirt or bodysuit under the bust and then fusing it to a fuller skirt. Try using contrasting colors and tying them together with some cute coordinating buttons on the bodice.

INDEX

© MELODIE MCDANIEL

Wendy Mullin has been sewing, pattern-making, and designing fabrics and graphics for more than twenty years. She is the founder and designer of the Built by Wendy clothing line, founded in 1991. Originally from suburban Chicago, she currently lives and works in New York City. For more about Wendy, check out her Web site at www.builtbywendy.com.

Beci Orpin is a designer-illustrator who lives in Melbourne, Australia, with her partner, Ralph, and son, Tyke. She has been creating designs for clients such as Built by Wendy, Bloom Cosmetics, and Burton Snowboards since 1997. In addition to designing her own clothing label, Princess Tina, she exhibits her artwork worldwide and has had shows in Australia, Japan, and the UK. For more about Beci, you can visit her Web site at www.beciorpin.com.

Eviana Hartman writes about culture in all its forms for such publications as *NYLON*, *Vogue*, *I.D.*, *Dwell*, and the *Washington Post*. In addition to collaborating with Wendy for the original *Sew U*, she was the chief writer for *Street: The NYLON Book of Global Style* (Universe, 2006). She lives in Brooklyn, New York, where she also spends time studying modern dance and photography, designing T-shirt graphics, and playing the synth.

Agnieszka Gasparska is the founder and creative director of NYC-based design studio Kiss Me I'm Polish. She received her BFA from the Cooper Union School of Art in 1999. Her design work has received recognition from publications such as *Time*, *Taschen*, and *Print*. Her clients have included the National Recording Academy, Lincoln Center, the Experience Music Project, Bloomberg, Knoll, and Fischerspooner. For more about Agnieszka, visit her Web site at www.kissmeimpolish.com.